Harold B. Smith, President, Christianity Today International

"Does the world truly need another leadership book? Yes, if that book is *Stewards of a Sacred Trust*. Building off a sense of Kingdom-calling that exists (or should exist!) between a board and a CEO and the ministry she or he leads, author and top executive and board veteran David McKenna delivers an extremely practical and powerfully challenging account detailing the God-led selection, transitioning, and development of leadership within the Christian context. The book compellingly charges all boards (and all would-be board members) to carefully weigh and work out the significance of their calling. And it offers deep hope and encouragement to any ministry leader who desires a leader whose commitment to her or his success is built upon prayer and their own sweat equity. A much-needed read—especially in these challenging times."

Leith Anderson, President, National Association of Evangelicals

"Who will lead our organizations into a better tomorrow? If we get this right, the future is bright. If we fail, the future is bleak. David McKenna shows us the way.

"We are at the beginning of a major leadership change in evangelical organizations from megachurches to universities to parachurch organizations. Some haven't chosen a top leader in decades. Others are looking for successors to founders. Dave McKenna brings stellar experience to coaching boards and selection committees to success in succession."

Steve Moore, Executive Director, The Murdock Trust

"In a time when much has been made about a 'generational transfer of wealth,' an even more significant 'generational transfer of leadership' is taking place in Christian organizations around the world. If the stewardship of the mission is the lifeblood of a board's responsibility, then the stewardship of the leadership selection, transition and nurture are the heartbeat of the board's covenant to those whom they serve. There are few others who have given us as careful thought to the principles and practices that are needed in this critical responsibility than David McKenna. I heartily recommend these resources to every board that wants to multiply their mission."

David Gyertson, Distinguished Professor of Leadership, Regent University

"The relationships between the CEO and the governing board are critical to the success and health of every organization. However, for Christ-centered organizations, those relationships witness the motivations and divine purposes at the heart of the entity's reason for being. David McKenna provides a compelling, practical and pastoral perspective on the nature and nurture of these relationships. Anchored in scriptural principles, informed by seasoned insight, and enlivened by real-world applications, McKenna challenges boards and CEOs to embrace their 'Sacred Trust' as stewards of their high calling in Christ Jesus. This is a must-have resource."

Dorothy Barbo, Professor Emeritus, The University of New Mexico Health Sciences Center and Chair, Presidential Search Committee for Asbury College, 2007

"The search for a new CEO is a challenging task. David McKenna has shared in this stepwise practical guide a workable process which can lead to a successful search and transition. His experience in multiple leadership positions and consulting in Christ-centered organizations has given him the knowledge and understanding of the needs of boards and search committees. There is no need to spend time reinventing this wheel. I have learned it works."

Stewards of a Sacred Trust

by DAVID L. MCKENNA

CEO Selection,
Transition and
Development for Boards
of Christ-centered Organizations

Stewards
of a
SACRED
TRUSt

ISBN-10: 1-936233-00-2
ISBN-13: 978-1-936233-00-7

Preface

Transitions are often some of the most important events in our individual lives and the lives of the organizations we serve. When a transition takes place there is greater risk of something radically going wrong than is the case in our normal daily routines. In my professional career, I have observed many such disasters that can affect organizations negatively for years, if not decades.

It appears that our culture is now heading into a time of significant transition and some would even say we are headed straight into a perfect storm that will radically affect Christ-centered organizations' ability to function. In a culture moving further and further from values grounded in biblical truth and morality, the "greatest" generation is moving off the scene; the massive baby boomer group (made up of many current CEOs and board members) is rapidly sliding into retirement; and a smaller pool of younger prospective leaders (often with different values) are coming up the ranks to take their place. Smooth and successful CEO selection, transition and development are key elements in relation to these changes.

For more than 30 years ECFA has been committed to helping Christ-centered organizations earn the public's trust by developing and maintaining standards of accountability that convey God-honoring ethical practices. As an accreditation agency dedicated to encouraging Christian ministries to earn the public's trust, ECFA has established standards that encompass financial accountability, fundraising, and board governance. One of the core elements of ECFA's ministry is providing ongoing capacity building for Christ-centered organizations in these three areas.

As the distance between the secular models of leadership and a Christian worldview increases, the need for successful transitions and training from a Christ-centered perspective intensifies. The secular perspectives are plentiful. However, little is available that pulls together professional excellence and spiritual discernment based on a biblical worldview. What is considered "Christian" is often a two-tiered view of leadership in which the Christian faith is simply overlaid on a secular premise. We believe that a Christ-centered ministry's ability to successfully manage the CEO selection, transition and development will strengthen the cause of Christ and significantly improve both the efficiency and effectiveness of many organizations.

If an executive officer is poorly selected, poorly trained and operating ineffectively, the weakness can derail an otherwise powerful force for the Kingdom of God. To meet these challenges, it is essential to increase organizational capacity at Christ-centered ministries by providing their CEOs and board members with the practical skills to lead in tumultuous times.

Because board governance and CEO training are so vital to the future health of Christ-centered organizations, I am delighted for ECFA to offer this book that draws on the rich experience, knowledge and spiritual insight of my friend, David McKenna. Over a period of more than 50 years, he served as president of three Christian institutions of higher education, chair of the board of two Christian universities, was founding chair of Christian College Consortium, board member of a wide range of Christ-centered organizations, and consultant for presidential searches, assessment and board development with a wide range of organizations.

My prayer is that God will use this book mightily as a tool to strengthen Christ-centered organizations in their efforts to fulfill the Great Commission.

Dan Busby
President
ECFA

Dedicated

to

Hugh A. White

Chair of the Board of
Spring Arbor College,
1957 to 1995

Mentor for my presidency

—

Model for my chairmanship

Table of Contents

Section III

Leading CEO Development

Author's Note

Why Do I Write?

After a lifetime of leadership in Christ-centered organizations as a president, board chair, trustee, and consultant, I write with the future in mind. Trends in society, government, business, education, and religion forecast unprecedented challenges for leaders of faith-affirming ministries. When crunch time comes, our response to these challenges will be based on the wisdom of an effective board and the maturity of an executive leader. For them, I write:

...as a **trustee** of a Christian university for nineteen years, with the last five as Chair of the Board (Spring Arbor University). During those years, we went through four presidential searches. Even though we turned the search process over to a representative campus committee and a search consultant, our board still held sole authority for the election of the president and sole responsibility for the outcome. Our accountability in this process is inescapable. I write because I see the need for trustees to understand fully the process.

...as a **director** on the board of many Christ-centered organizations ranging from local ministries to international missions. In this capacity, I witnessed chief executive officer (CEO) transition in almost every form, from the lockstep of family succession to the wild machinations of political scrambles. Strange as it seems, directors often assumed that the ministry would fly on automatic pilot when ambiguity and anxiety threatened the stability and spirit of an organization. I write with the conviction that the board has a special responsibility in the time of transition for leading with consistency, communication, and creativity.

...as a **president** for three institutions of Christian higher education (Spring Arbor University, Seattle Pacific University, and Asbury Theological Seminary) over a period of thirty-three years.

Early in my career, I made the choice between the presidency of a large state university and a small Christian college. It was a choice of love. After being elected as president, however, I sensed the board saying, "Congratulations, now you are on your own." Yes, the board gave me full support for personal and professional development, but the initiative was my own. I write because board governance includes responsibility for nurturing the gifts of CEO leadership as a maturing model for personal and professional development throughout the organization.

...as a **consultant** to CEO searches in both Christian higher education and other evangelical organizations. While professional standards for CEO searches apply to all organizations, religious or secular, I am convinced that the Christ-centered organization requires a highly-selective search process sensitive to the nuances of theology, history, and mission that give our ministries their character and their culture. In the CEO search process presented in this book, I have witnessed the special meaning of participatory governance as directors, administrators, staff, and stakeholders from the constituency come together as the Body of Christ. Even with varying viewpoints, we learn to work together, respect each other, and come to unified decisions. When the search is over and the candidate has been selected for presentation to the board, the committee members are bonded as colleagues, friends, brothers and sisters, and the ministry itself has become part of a "learning organization." From this perspective comes the highest motivation for my writing. As a consultant, I have witnessed this transformation and want to see it happen again and again.

For Whom Do I Write?

Genuine love and intimate involvement in the life and ministry of Christ-centered organizations prompted me to write this book. The range extends from small local ministries surviving on economic shoestrings to megalith global ministries flourishing on multi-million dollar budgets. They have one main thing in common: a governing board with responsibility for CEO leadership. This is the fundamental relationship that determines their effectiveness no matter how diverse they may be. At the very center of this relationship is the board's responsibility for the selection, transition, and development of CEO leadership. In every case, the working principles are the same even though they are selectively applied within different organizational models and environmental settings. This book is for all of these:

- **parachurch boards** operating on a business model and asking for CEO leadership that will integrate their mission with the expectations of a Christ-centered organization;

- **denominational boards,** local, national, and international, whose ecclesiastical authority and discipline directly influence the selection, transition, and development of pastoral leadership, with the challenge of changing expectations from their constituency; and

- **independent church boards** adjusting from the influence of a founding personality to the requirements of a governing body, an administrative structure, and an accountable senior pastor.

It is the wide scope of these needs that prompted me to write *Stewards of a Sacred Trust: CEO Selection, Transition and Development for Boards of Christ-centered Organizations.* The book is written in a three parts:

Section I—Overseeing CEO Selection;

Section II—Managing CEO Transition, and

Section III—Leading CEO Development.

After each chapter in these sections is a checklist entitled "With All Due Diligence." These checklists will aid board members of Christ-centered organizations to fulfill their responsibility to oversee the search, transition, and development of our CEO.

The process and the instrument, however, are only a means to an end. In the Christ-centered organization, trust is a two-sided coin. One side is God's trust in us to steward the rare gifts of executive leadership; the other is our trust in each other to build the board-CEO relationship as a model for the whole community. When this trust is sealed by the presence of the Spirit of God, it is indeed, our sacred trust.

David L. McKenna

Chapter 1

A Christ-centered Viewpoint

Let's begin with the timely question: "What is a board's stewardship responsibility for the leadership selection, transition, and development of its CEO?" To answer this question, we must ask another question, "What does it mean to be Christ-centered—as an organization—in our stewardship as members of its board, and in our responsibility for the development of our CEO?" These are questions begging for the application of faith that leads to wholeness.

The Christ-centered Organization

Most people know what we mean by "faith-based" organizations. It tends to become a political term. Across the broad spectrum of religious ministries, faith-based organizations are nonprofit entities with a motivation for some form of public service to the community and often having some kind of support from governmental agencies.

Most people also have an idea about the meaning of "Christian" organizations. It has to be an historical term. They envision a ministry with roots in the Judeo-Christian tradition, whether a group that keeps its Christian identity in name alone (YMCA) or one whose statement of faith and practice is unequivocally Christian (The Salvation Army).

What, then, do we mean by a "Christ-centered" organization?

Every organization has a driving force at the core that determines its identity and establishes its character. In secular organizations, the driving force may be professional expertise, market share, technology, research, service, or profit. A Christ-centered organization will not be exempt from the influence of these factors, but they cannot be the driving force. It is the mind and spirit of Jesus Christ as revealed in the Word of God and enacted through the agency of the Holy Spirit that drives the Christ-centered organization—from the inside out. Seen in its vision, stated in its mission, and felt in its tone, the mind and spirit of Jesus Christ defines its identity and shapes its character.

A "Christ-centered organization" is not an exclusive term because "faith-based" and "Christian" organizations may also be "Christ-centered." Integration of Christ's principles as revealed in the Word of God and infused by the Holy Spirit defines the difference. Frank Gaberlein, my mentor, gave an analogy that illustrates the idea. He said that we must drive deep our stake of commitment in Jesus Christ in order to let the tether of influence and action reach out to the full circumference of our life and ministry. If the stake is firm, the tether can be long, but if the stake is wobbly, the tether that plays out too far will pull up the stake.

Apply this analogy to the definition of a Christ-centered organization. If the stake is firm at center, it can play out in spirit and discipline to the farthest reaches of the ministry. Specifically applied, the mind and spirit of Christ must be the integrating center that penetrates and pervades every thought and action of the organization. No one pretends that this is easy, but if we accept Paul's organic model for the Body of Christ in I Corinthians 12:12-31, we have to admit that it is possible. A Christ-centered organization will have structural clarity, division of labor, assignment of roles, and use of gifts working together with the mind of Christ and brought to life by the Spirit of Christ. The key, of course, is interpersonal relationships. They start with the connection between Christ the Head and the members of His Body. The proof of these connections is in the relationships among the members of the Body of Christ. To be effective, the organization must have different roles for its members, but not in a hierarchy of status that elevates some and demeans others. Each member is esteemed as a contributor to the organization with equal concern for the other.

A Christ-centered board is distinct from other nonprofit boards in four ways:

1. **Common Christian faith.** The board members should all be mature Christians following Jesus Christ. These are people involved in prayerful intercession and act in faith and in integrity in all they do in their personal and professional lives.

2. **Statement of Christian faith.** A Christ-centered organization has a statement of faith that all board members support as a basis for all decisions made by the board. These faith commitments provide the values and theological framework for all decisions made by the board.

3. **Christian worldview.** As a result of the board members common Christian faith and the organization's written Statement of Faith, the board seeks to operate from a Christian worldview. This means that board members acknowledge God as the Creator and Sustainer of life and that God's eternal kingdom is the ultimate purpose of our existence. The focus of a Christ-centered organization, therefore, is to seek to accomplish the Great Commission as outlined in the Bible.

4. **A maturing fellowship.** As members of the Body of Christ, each member of the board of a Christ-centered organization is committed to caring for each other, learning and growing together, creating a climate for personal, professional and spiritual growth for every employee of the ministry, and demonstrating love to all whom they serve.

5. **Accountable to God as stewards.** As a result of these four assumptions, ECFA and its board members are accountable to God, Who provides the moral authority for all that is done.

With this understanding that God owns all, board members serve as stewards of God's creation and are accountable to God. The board member's actions, plans, and policies are ultimately responsible for reflecting God's Will for the organization. Board members should remember that Jesus Christ is our Possessor and our Dispossessor. He ordains, sustains, and blesses. The organization belongs entirely to God. Prayerful deliberation then becomes the norm and not the exception.

Organizational studies back up the practical outcomes of this biblical model for the Christ-centered organization. With the mind and spirit of Christ as its integrating center, the Christ-centered organization is a dynamic movement toward wholeness: (a) All of its members are personally committed to Jesus Christ and to the outworking of the Great Commission in the purpose of the organization; (b) All of its members find meaning in their lives and satisfaction in their work by being a partner in the ministry with all other members; and (c) All of its members are motivated by the redemptive hope of seeing God's Will done in the contemporary world and anticipating His coming in glory.

Christ-centered Stewardship

Primary responsibility for setting the policies of the Christ-centered organization rests with the members of its governing board. For good reason, they are often called "trustees" because they are charged to hold in trust all of the resources given to them by God. "Stewards" conveys the same meaning but with biblical roots. In the original language, "stewards" meant "householders" who managed all of the affairs of the household. The term makes a clear distinction between "ownership" and "stewardship." While everything belongs to the owner of the household, the steward owns nothing. Yet the owner (God) trusts the steward with management of all that He has and holds the steward accountable for all that He owns. For the Christ-centered organization, therefore, the biblical definition of a steward

4

determines the role of the board in every facet of its governing role. Owner of nothing, manager of all, and accountable for all sums up what it means to be on the board of a Christ-centered organization.

The Christ-centered Board-CEO Relationship

Among all of the relationships in the Christ-centered organization, the key connector is between the board and the CEO, more specifically, between the board chair and the CEO. The soul of the organization depends upon this primary relationship. In the original language, "soul" and "throat" are synonymous words. The throat is not only the physical connector between the head and the body, it is the two-way passage for instructions from the brain and feelings from the nerves at the same time that air from the lungs and blood from the heart are going to the head. Following this analogy, the soul of the Christ-centered organization can be read by the thoughts and feelings of the mind of Christ and the breath and blood of the Spirit of Christ.

The board-CEO relationship is the soul of the Christ-centered organization. It connects leaders to followers, communicates vision and mission to the body, and sets the tone for the organization. At the same time, it perceives the strength and vitality of the organization that flows from the body back to the head. To read the quality of the Christ-centered organization, check the quality of the board-CEO relationship. Be even more specific. Check the relationship between the board chair and the CEO. This is where it all begins. If the board and its chair are committed to the growth and development of their executive leader, the message ripples through the whole organization. From the integral point of the board and board chair-CEO relationship, the spiritual health of the organization is created.

Christ-centered CEO Leadership

Study after study tells us that the key to leadership development is a board that supports and challenges its CEO. Follow-up studies add the fact that the board must be strategically engaged and intimately present in the life cycle of selecting, transitioning, and developing its leader. For Christ-centered organizations, this relationship is more than effective governance; it is testimony to the role of the board as stewards of the rare gift of CEO leadership in the name and for the sake of Jesus Christ.

Christ-centered CEO leadership is evidence of the mind and spirit of Christ wholly integrated into our character and competence. In an introductory course in theology, the professor illustrated his lecture on holiness by pulling a thread from his blue serge suit. Holding it to light, he said, "Holiness is like this. Every thread of our being will have the tone and texture of the whole cloth." His analogy awakened in me the understanding of holiness as wholeness and created in me an insatiable thirst for the presence of His Spirit in every part of my character and in every expression of my competence. That thirst has never been quenched and the desire to bring every thought and action into obedience with the mind of Christ is my consuming desire. The irony is that the closer we get to God, the more unworthy we feel and the more we confess our need to be holy. When we talk about CEO leadership, we are not talking about perfection, we are talking about progress. As the mind and spirit of Christ are integrated into the character of the CEO, the move toward maturity will be evident in a good reputation, practical wisdom, and spiritual-mindedness, the same qualities for which the seven deacons were elected in Acts 6.

Wholeness comes into focus in CEO leadership because this is the fulcrum upon which the future of the Christ-centered organization is balanced. Yet CEO leadership development does not stand alone. The environment of the parent organization, the principle of biblical stewardship, and the investment of the board in its CEO must all work together as holistic, Christ-centered threads in a seamless garment. The beauty of this relationship is that the Christ-centered organization does not have to wear its faith on its sleeve. It will be a well-defined structure governed by clear policies and fair practices, meeting the highest level of professional standards, and being fully accountable in the public eye. But if you pull a thread from any part of the cloth, it will have the texture of truth and the tone of grace. On the wall of the boardroom or executive office of every Christ-centered organization, the words of Micah Network's *Declaration on Integral Mission* might well be a constant reminder: "As in the life of Jesus, being, doing and saying are at the heart of our integral task."

In this book, we put this same passion into print as we see the mind and spirit of Christ permeating the whole and creating the distinctive character of the Christ-centered organization, its board, and its executive leader.

Overseeing CEO Selection

Chapter 2

Overseeing CEO Selection
A Refining Process

A Christ-centered organization can write its history in chapters named for its leaders. Whether the era of a leader is short or long, a success or a failure, there is an imprint that will not go away. For good reason, then, when the board of a Christ-centered organization faces the task of finding its next CEO, its members have come to a defining moment when the destiny of the ministry is in their hands. As such, board members are "fate holders" as well as stakeholders in the future of their organization. The extra responsibility weighs down when the board realizes that the search is so selective and the top prospects are so few. Add the fact that most boards are unprepared for leadership transition and at a loss to know how to conduct the search. Consequently, the task is turned over to a search committee and a search consultant. However, the board cannot delegate its responsibility for the quality of the process and the selection of the person.

This book is written expressly to help boards understand what is involved in finding its CEO, monitoring the process as it goes forward, and assuring its sole authority for the outcome. The complexity of the process requires professional guidance, and even then, there are always unexpected happenings that call for experienced judgment. This book is intended to be a resource for board members of Christ-centered organizations who take seriously their responsibility for oversight of such a momentous decision.

Visualizing the Process

Think of finding your next CEO as a refining process, like the work of a silversmith taking the raw ore of precious metal and producing a delicate instrument of invaluable worth. The search committee, often under the guidance of a consultant, serves as the master craftsman for the process, accepting its formal authority from the board (Step 1), setting search goals that are consistent with its mission (Step 2), developing solemn charges for all participants in the process (Step 3), and preparing a profile of personal and professional qualifications needed to lead the ministry to the next level of its strategic plan (Step 4). With the plan for the refining process in place, individuals with rare leadership gifts represent the raw material for the search. Thus, the process advances to identify and recruit a selective pool of qualified prospects for the CEO position (Step 5). The refining heat of the crucible is the theological, historical, missional, and strategic context for the ministry of the Christ-centered organization. Out of these priorities, the Leadership Profile becomes the die through which the gifts, experience and potential of prospective candidates are passed (Step 6). Under the white heat of the crucible, those whose leadership gifts are not a match for the present and future needs of the ministry will be eliminated. In the end, only one candidate will come through the rigorous shaping for presentation to the board (Step 7). Before that, however, there is the final step in the refining process when the silversmith hand-rubs the precious product to give it a special glow. In the case of CEO selection for the Christ-centered organization, it is the Holy Spirit Who finishes the process and puts the glow of His presence upon this person and the decision (Step 8).

Refining Steps

Analogies are never perfect, but when it comes to finding your next CEO, the refining process comes closest. Imagine the refining process as the converging lines of a deep "V." The wide open-ended top represents the mouth where the pieces of planning and

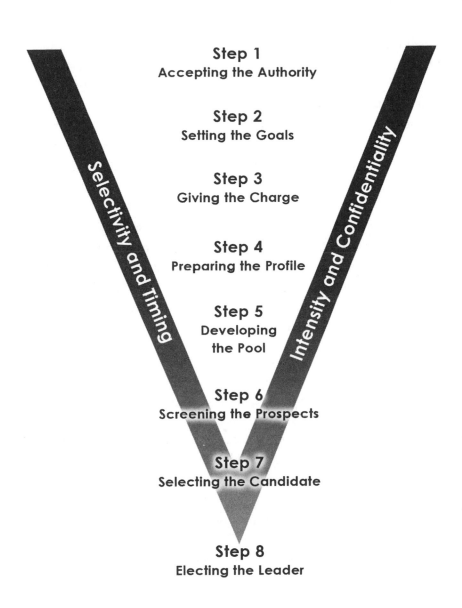

Step 1
Accepting the Authority

Step 2
Setting the Goals

Step 3
Giving the Charge

Step 4
Preparing the Profile

Step 5
Developing
the Pool

Step 6
Screening the Prospects

Step 7
Selecting the Candidate

Step 8
Electing the Leader

Selectivity and Timing

Intensity and Confidentiality

organizing go into the search process. From there, the sides narrow as the search progresses until converging at the pointed end when the executive leader is elected. Within this "V" are the eight steps of the refining process.

The converging lines of the "V" symbolize essential characteristics of a quality search. *Selectivity* increases as the number of prospects is reduced. *Timing* will also be critical as the search progresses. During the planning stage, there is value in taking the time to complete preparations before proceeding. As the search progresses, time between steps will be shortened to respect the schedule of candidates and reduce the risk of unfortunate leaks of personal information. *Intensity* also increases as the process narrows toward a conclusion. General questions become personalized inquiries and general references become in-depth checks. *Confidentiality* must be carefully protected in the latter stages of the search. Especially in cases of delicate negotiations with top candidates, the pledge of confidence is all-important. Finally, the lines of *commitment* converge for both the candidates and the search committee. As the candidate becomes more committed to the possibility of serving as leader of the organization, the search committee's commitment to the candidate as their prospective leader must be equally clear.

Like the process of refining raw ore into an instrument of beauty, CEO selection is a work of engineering and a work of art. An engineer inspects the details of the search process at close range and an artist steps back to see the whole picture. What better way to describe the Spirit of God at work through human instruments? Board members of Christ-centered organizations will see this model at work in all of our deliberations and decisions. Whether selecting a new CEO, setting policies for governance, stewarding financial resources, approving program proposals, or grappling with complex legal or moral issues, the Spirit of God will keep us balanced between the precision of the engineer and the perspective of the artist.

With All Due Diligence
Board Check
A Refining Process

As you have observed or participated in the search process for CEO leadership in a Christ-centered organization, do you feel as if your board will:

	Yes	No
1. sense the full weight of its responsibility?	_____	_____
2. foresee the highly selective nature of the search?	_____	_____
3. fully understand the complexity of the search process?	_____	_____
4. adopt a systematic plan with clarity, precision, and progressive steps?	_____	_____
5. maintain oversight for the process?	_____	_____
6. witness the coherence of system and Spirit in the final result?	_____	_____
7. function as both engineer and artist in overseeing the process?	_____	_____
8. give the process and participants highest priority in faithful and fervent prayer?	_____	_____

Chapter 3

Overseeing CEO Selection
Accepting Sole Authority

I f board members took an oath of office, we would first swear to "preserve and advance the mission of the organization." In almost the same breath, we would then pledge to "accept the responsibility for the election of the CEO as our solemn duty and sacred trust." We know that the selection of the CEO is one of the most important decisions a board can make, but how does it qualify as a solemn duty and sacred trust?

A Solemn Duty

Whenever the board gathers in session, an air of anticipation mingles with a weighty sense of responsibility. Duty calls for decisions on policy, people and programs that determine the destiny of the organization. Among these decisions, the selection of the CEO stands alone for several reasons.

First and foremost, the board has *sole authority* for the election of the CEO. Even though the board may appoint their members to the search committee, approve other members who represent the organization and the constituency, and hire a consultant to guide the process, the board cannot delegate its final authority. No one else will be held accountable for the selection of the CEO. The buck stops there.

Our sense of solemn duty deepens when we remember that the CEO is *the only employee* of the board. The transfer to the CEO of full authority and accountability for the administration of the organization is a momentous decision of total trust. Although the CEO is subject to personal and public opinion from every sector and occasionally evaluated by constituent surveys or consultant review, none of it counts unless the board considers these assessments in their own deliberations.

An even greater sense of solemn duty grips us when we remember that the board shares its *primary responsibility* for the "preservation and advancement of the mission" with the CEO. Of course, the criteria for the search of the CEO begins with the personal commitment of all candidates to the mission of the organization. But we also know that the CEO has the leverage of a thousand subtle means to reshape, refine, and revise the mission. Again, total trust is at stake. Whenever a board elects its CEO, it is a casting a vote for the future of the mission as well.

A Sacred Trust

Election of the CEO separates Christ-centered organizations from other organizations because it is a sacred trust. While the professional standards for the search process must be the same for all organizations, Christ-centered organizations have a spiritual dimension that cannot be denied. For good reason, "cookie cutter consulting" should be vigorously resisted on presidential search in Christ-centered organizations. Likewise, attempts to spiritualize the process at the expense of professional integrity cannot be tolerated. To put our sacred trust into perspective, think on these things.

Christ-centered organizations are *God-ordained ministries.* That means if our faith-based ministries did not exist, they would have to be invented. Christ-centered organizations are "vines of God's own planting." From the beginning of Christian history, the Church has had what we now call "parachurch" ministries that serve alongside of traditional ecclesiastical structures. While not legally connected to a larger faith body, they complement and reinforce ministries, focusing upon compassion on a global scale. They also garner support from a wider evangelical spectrum. Without a doubt, they are also Christ-centered organizations.

Ask the question of any Christ-centered organization: "If it did not exist, would it have to be invented?" For any God-ordained ministry (duplicating and competing organizations notwithstanding), the answer will be a resounding "Yes."

The sacred trust of Christ-centered organizations is further confirmed when the board elects a leader *called of God* to be CEO. It is different to elect a person who accepts the position after weighing the merits of alternative offers than the candidate whose commitment comes with a clear sense of divine calling. When the board of a Christ-centered ministry elects a CEO, a covenant of eternal proportions is created. Just as the CEO offers leadership gifts, the board accepts its responsibility for stewarding those gifts. Together, they enter a sacred trust with full and final accountability to God Himself.

Finally, we remember the *eternal impact* of CEO leadership. Whether the Christ-centered organization is large or small, members of the professional and service staffs stake their lives on the leader whom the board elects. Moreover, millions of people served by Christ-centered ministries are affected by the quality of that leadership. Like the ripple effect of a stone tossed into a pond, the CEO's influence will move in waves through generations. No decision of the board, absolutely no decision, is more profound.

For good reason, then, the search process for the CEO must be bathed in prayer. Perfunctory prayers to open the meetings are not enough. Led by the search chair, committee members need to wait before God, reflect on the meaning of biblical leadership, confess their need for God's guidance, and ask for the discerning mind of the Holy Spirit. Their prayers need to be bolstered by the prayers of the staff and the external constituency, even joining together in designated days for prayer and fasting. A consecration service for the appointed committee members in conjunction with a board meeting confirms the sacredness of the search.

A Personal Invitation

In electing a CEO, the board must exercise responsibility through a search process for which they have full responsibility but not complete control. Typically, the full board is directly involved only at the beginning and the end of the process. Yet oversight is a responsibility that cannot be forfeited. To ask the right questions, exercise the responsibilities of oversight, and cast an informed vote in the final decision, board members need to understand the process of search and the principles of selection. I invite you to join me in thinking through a proven process customized for the Christ-centered organization. The purpose is to help you in the solemn duty and sacred trust for the most important decision that board members are called to make.

With All Due Diligence
Board Check
Accepting Sole Authority

When the time comes for our board to activate the search process for a new CEO, are we prepared for the task by:

	Yes	No
1. viewing the process as a solemn duty within our sacred trust:		
a. confirming our God-ordained ministry?	_____	_____
b. seeking a leader called of God?	_____	_____
c. realizing its eternal impact?	_____	_____
2. making it clear to all that the board has sole authority for the election of its CEO?	_____	_____
3. making it clear to all the CEO is the only employee of the board?	_____	_____
4. seeing our primary role as partnering with the CEO to preserve and advance the mission and ministry of the organization?	_____	_____
5. supporting the search process with a climate of corporate and personal prayer?	_____	_____

6. accepting responsibility for CEO
   search even if delegating responsibility
   to a search committee and engaging
   an outside consultant by

   a. understanding the process? _____ _____

   b. approving the process? _____ _____

   c. maintaining oversight over the
      process? _____ _____

Chapter 4

Overseeing CEO Selection Setting Missional Goals

A board seldom, if ever, looks forward to a CEO search which is so critical to the life of the organization and so costly in time, money, and energy. Even before a search committee is formed, the search chair is named and the search charge is given, the board needs to see that finding its next leader is a window of opportunity. Through that window, affirmative goals can be set that will advance the mission of the organization, provide the framework for leadership expectations, and create the climate for transformational change in the organization itself.

The Spiritual Goal

Christ-centered organizations are distinguished by their commitment to the will of God permeating every phase of mission and ministry. The presidential search process is an unusual opportunity to demonstrate that commitment by setting the goal of *assuring a process that works in concert with the will of God*. Even though the process is directed by standards common to all professional organizations, board members in Christ-centered ministries pray for guidance from the all-encompassing mind and spirit of God. Everyone involved in the search—whether board members, administrators, staff, consultant or constituents—must come together under that commitment.

As a person who has been in all four corners of presidential search, as board member, board chair, presidential candidate and search consultant, I remember these experiences as *"kairos"* moments when diverse lines of interest converged in concert with the Will of God. Time and again, I have seen search chairs suddenly show uncanny wisdom in resolving sticky issues, or committee members marvel at an unexpected unity of mind and the whole organization join together in a time of celebration. If we begin presidential search with the spiritual goal of seeing God at work, He is faithful.

The Leadership Goal

There are two sides to the coin of presidential search. On one side is a clear statement of the organization's needs, present and future. On the other side are people with gifts to meet those needs. The question is: How do we bring these organizational needs and individual gifts together? The answer is in the leadership goal of *selecting the best person whose leadership gifts match the present and projected needs of our Christ-centered organization.*

A focused search disciplined by a rigorous and Spirit-guided process must follow to meet this goal. Political pressure and personal sentiment have to be put aside to assure the integrity of the process and the election of the best candidate. It is an unforgettable experience to see widespread differences between needs and gifts begin to narrow as the process cancels some candidates and advances others toward the goal. While the match is never perfect, there is no substitute for the exhilaration of an "Aha!" experience when the individual gifts of the best candidate mesh with organizational needs and goals.

The Planning Goal

If a Christ-centered organization is on the move, it will have a strategic plan initiated by the CEO with input from constituents, reviewed and affirmed by the board. There is always the danger that the plan will become a document etched in stone, but if done properly, it gives the organization a target on future goals with flexibility for change. Accordingly, the planning goal for the search process is *relating the priorities for leadership gifts to the strategic goals of the organization.*

The search process is severely handicapped if there is disconnection between leadership priorities and strategic goals. In some cases, the qualifications of the candidate are so dazzling that the strategic goals are forgotten. In other cases, the strategic goals are so fixed that they override the potential of the candidates. The task of the search committee is to use the strategic plan as a long-term guidance system for presidential priorities without limiting the options on either side of the equation.

The Public Relations Goal

The CEO search process is a boon for public relations. It is a rare moment when the organization's vision, mission and identity can be communicated far and wide through position announcements, religious networks, public media, and word of mouth. Our public relations goal, then, is to use the CEO search *for communicating broadly the vision, mission, and identity of our Christ-centered organization and assuring goodwill with all participants in the process.*

So often, public relations is a dull tool in the CEO search. Communications, in particular, need to be honed so that a coordinated plan of public information can be implemented through dedicated websites, focused advertising, news releases, free media outlets, and formal press conferences in step with the search plan itself.

Once these goals are set for the search process, everything else falls into line. From the board's initial charge to the search committee to the final moment when the new leader is announced, every step in the process must be consistent with these goals.

With All Due Diligence
Board Check
Setting the Goals

As the first step in preparation for executive search, has the board agreed upon these goals that will guide the process?

	Yes	No
1. Spiritual goal—to follow and work in concert with the will of God	_____	_____
2. Leadership goal—to select the best person with the best fit for the presidency	_____	_____
3. Planning goal—to match the priorities for leadership with the strategic goals of the organization	_____	_____
4. Public relations goal—to communicate the vision, mission and identity of the organization within the constituency and to the general public	_____	_____

Chapter 5

Overseeing CEO Selection
Sharing the Trust

Corporate bylaws often give the charge to the board of a Christ-centered organization "to elect the Chief Executive Officer." This is like a lodestar for navigating the search process. All other charges flow from this initial charge to the board. All participants in the search process, whether board chair or member of the search committee, function under the aegis of this charge. Nothing can go beyond its mandate or deviate from its authority.

Charge to the Board

A CEO search usually begins when the full board charges a search committee with responsibility to *organize and manage the search process by appointing a search chair, commissioning a search committee, possibly engaging a consultant, approving the search plan and preparing the search budget.* All committee recommendations or actions should be confirmed or acted upon by the full board.

Special attention goes to preparing a budget for the CEO search. Board members assume it is a necessary expense but seldom realize how much it costs. Two budgets are recommended. One is the *search budget,* including expenses for search committee meetings, search assistant's salary, consultant fees, candidate travel, and office costs. A *transition budget* is also needed. This budget projects the cost of leadership change involving the expenses of a transition committee, funding the costs incurred in compensating, and bidding farewell to the departing CEO, paying an interim executive (if applicable), bringing the new leader on board—including moving, housing and costs of the inaugural celebration. Tens of thousands of dollars can escalate into six figures. Because of the implications of these one-time expenses, search and transition budgets are urgent items on the agenda of the board committee managing them.

Charge to the Board Chair

The question always arises, "Should the chair of the board be the chair of the search committee?" No answer is cut and dried, but the preference is that the board chair should *not* be the search chair. The reasons are manifold. The board chair has his or her hands full with the responsibilities for developing and implementing policies and assuring continuity with the departing or interim CEO. Furthermore, the board chair often has a role in the search process which may include *serving as an ex officio member of the search committee, advising the committee, offering the board's perspective, helping resolve committee conflicts, making critical contacts with candidates, developing a relationship with the finalists, and negotiating the terms of agreement with a prospective CEO.* Without detracting from the authority of the search chair, there may be occasions when the board chair can step in to make a difference. Whether it is speaking with another board chair related to the candidate, answering questions for prospects, encouraging a decision from a key candidate, or negotiating the terms of a contractual agreement, the board chair generally has significant opportunities to positively contribute to the search process without chairing the search committee.

Charge to the Search Committee Chair

The appointment of the search chair by the board is a decision second only to the election of the CEO in the search process. In order to confirm the authority and oversight of the board, the search chair should be a member of the board itself. Along with the appointment goes the charge to *preside over the search committee, assure the integrity of its process, communicate its progress, officially represent the organization in contacts and negotiations with candidates, and lead the committee to an affirmative recommendation to the board for the election of the CEO.*

Work and wisdom along with commitment are the invaluable resources that a search chair must bring to the process. Work involves the dedication of timeless hours leading the committee, processing applications and communicating with candidates. Before accepting the role of chair, a person should realize that the task will have high priority for a period of six months or more. In this period will be critical times when everything else must be put aside.

The job entails a thorough understanding of the character of the organization, in-depth experience with its dynamics, and Spirit-guided maturity in decision-making. All of these resources will come into play as the search chair guides a diverse committee through the complicated process with a wide-ranging pool of prospects to choosing a single candidate. After the search committee concludes its work, the search chair has one more duty. A review and evaluation of the search process should be written for organizational history with suggestions for future search committees. As the person most intimately involved in the process and people, the search chair is the logical author of that record. The quality of the search and its outcome rests heavily upon the shoulders of the search chair.

Charge to the Search Committee

A board takes the ultimate risk when it delegates its authority to a search committee charged with CEO selection. The track record for Christ-centered organizations, however, confirms that a common commitment to Christ and His Kingdom makes the risk worthwhile.

The charge to a search committee and its members is *to attend all meetings, make your membership a spiritual calling, bring the perspective of those you represent to the process, participate fully in the discussions, contribute to civil discourse, maintain complete confidence, learn how to check references, review and rate candidates according to the Leadership Profile, and seek the mind of God in the final decision to present a candidate to the board.*

Much can be said about the responsibility of the committee's members. First, determine that the majority of the committee is made up of members of the board, including the search chair. Search committees with no more than an odd number of nine or eleven members work best. If a vote of the committee is tied, it is the committee chair who will cast the deciding vote.

A Christ-centered organization is unique because its life's blood flows through staff members who are called of God to serve sacrificially in the ministry. Its continuing existence depends upon constituents who keep this source of life flowing. As partners with the board to advance the mission of the organization, they deserve a place at the table in the search for new leadership. If, for instance, a search committee of nine members includes a majority of five board members, there are four positions left for internal and external representatives. They must be carefully selected for their commitment to the organization, their perspective on leadership and their professional expertise. The search process becomes an unusual opportunity for bonding the board, staff and constituents in a common cause. Whatever decision is made about the committee's composition, the board needs to specify the number and kind of representatives in its original charge.

Incumbent CEOs often wonder about their role in the search for their successor. Wisdom says that they should never be members or advisors to the search committee. They do, however, deserve periodic briefings from the search chair and under a pledge of confidentiality, can be a valuable resource for assessing candidates.

A single statement bonds committee members in a pledge of confidentiality. From the moment of appointment, the pressure is on. Friends want an inside tip and colleagues expect that a professional relationship overrides the pledge of confidentiality. But nothing should be allowed to break the pledge. Those willing to submit their names as candidates put themselves as the highest risk. For example, one of the nation's most sought educators was about to be presented to the board for election at a top-ranking research university when his name was leaked to the press and became headline news. He immediately withdrew because of this violation of confidence.

The pledge of confidentiality made by all participants in the search process is supported by the systems used as part of the search process. If an outside consultant is used, contacts with candidates might be funneled through the consultant to ensure confidentiality. If the search is handled without using an outside consultant, it will be important to determine how candidates may confidentially communicate with the search committee and how electronic and paper communications will be securely maintained. It may be important to establish a temporary post office box and a separate email address to enhance confidentiality.

Charge to the Search Consultant

One of the first questions that comes up when a board must select a new CEO is, "Do we need a search consultant?" The answer is not unequivocally "Yes." If a Christ-centered organization has the advantage of a person on the board or in the staff who is well-schooled in executive search, a potential search chair who is willing to give top priority to implementing the process, and a unified team of board, staff and constituent representatives who are ready to work on designated assignments, a search consultant may not be needed. Such resources of time, energy and expertise are so rare that few ministries can qualify for exception. Even when these resources are available, there is merit in having

- the objectivity of a process consultant to keep the search on track and deal with sensitive issues, or

- a consultant who specializes in some aspect of the search process, such as executive networking, reference checking, psychological testing or legal matters relating to credentials, and responding to applicants who are not finalists in the search process.

Because most searches in Christ-centered organizations have benefited from the services of a consultant who guides the whole search process from beginning to end, the following charge is written with the full service consultant in mind. It is expected that the professional consultant will accept the charge to *guide the search process, represent the search committee in identifying, contacting, referencing and presenting prospects for candidacy with professional skill, personal integrity, and spiritual understanding, and assure the effectiveness of the search committee in fulfilling its charge.*

Guidelines for interviewing and retaining a search consultant include:

1. **Spiritual compatibility.** Christ-centered organizations are especially favored to have a choice of search firms of national reputation headed by spiritually mature leaders who see their consulting role as a call to ministry. From among these choices, the search committee will want to choose the one with whom there is a blending of mind and spirit in order to accomplish the spiritual goal of assuring a process that works in concert with the will of God.

2. **Missional sensitivity.** No two Christ-centered organizations are the same. Historical, theological, and cultural affirmations and nuances create a character that is unique to itself. A good search consultant is always a good salesperson, but a search committee needs to get behind the pitch in order to find the firm that best understands and resonates with that character.

3. **Relational connection.** As always, the key to selection of a search firm is the relational fit between the consultant, search chair, and search committee. Interviews with more than one search consultant will be like a "sniff test" on the future working relationship. Central to the decision will be the chemistry between the search chair and the search consultant. The analogy

of a football coach and a quarterback helps us see the relationship. The consultant is like a coach who creates the game plan, calls most of the plays, gets the players ready to play, manages the clock, and inspires the team to win. The quarterback leads the team on the field, calls the plays, scopes the field, adjusts with audibles, and hands off or passes the ball on every play. Whether in a football game or executive search, coordination of leadership and execution by the team make the winning combination.

4. **Customized process.** Every Christ-centered organization is unique with differences in organizational, personal, and interpersonal dynamics that directly influence the search process. A cookie cutter process or a boilerplate CEO profile that ignores these differences is sufficient reason for rejecting a prospective search consultant.

5. **Selective approach.** CEO selection for a Christ-centered organization is a highly selective process. The criterion for an effective search in these ministries is not the breadth of the net that is spread or the number of candidates who are brought to the table. It is creating a selective pool of mission-matched persons who have become candidates through a targeted approach and a personalized process.

6. **Cost-effective budgeting.** Cost of consultant services is always a consideration that needs to be guided by stewardship principles. A full-service consultant usually works on a set fee based upon a percentage of CEO compensation. When expenses are added, the total cost will represent a major investment for the board in consultant services. But, as so many Christ-centered organizations have learned from painful experience, when the mission of the organization and the destiny of an individual are at stake, it is far better to spend the dimes on the front end of CEO search rather than dollars on the back end of CEO failure. Still, cost-conscious ministries supported by sacrificial dollars have a particular responsibility for good stewardship

in developing the CEO search budget. A negotiated flat fee plus expenses is standard for executive search consultants. Contingency, hourly, and open-ended arrangements should be avoided. As part of the interviews for prospective consultants, it is most appropriate to ask, "How can you assist us in exercising our stewardship responsibility by a cost-effective search process within our budget?"

7. **Search references.** Most search firms have a track record for results because sooner or later, a CEO appointment has to be made. The quality of the search and the success of the selected CEO, however, may vary widely. Prospective search consultants should have no problem providing references for searches done in similar or related Christ-centered ministry. Frank questions should be asked, such as, "What do you consider your most successful search consultation? Why was it successful? What do you see to be the reason for searches to flounder or ever fail? Have you had such an experience? What did you learn from it and what would you do differently? What three Christ-centered organizations where you have consulted on the CEO search would serve as your references? May we check with other Christ-centered ministries of our choice where you have served as a consultant?" If a prospective consultant is uneasy with hard questions, it is all the more reason to check references in depth.

8. **Image transfer.** Boards of Christ-centered organizations take a risk when engaging a search consultant because that person will temporarily become the face of the ministry. Credibility is at stake in the spiritual maturity, personal integrity, professional demeanor, and interpersonal skills of the consultant. The final question that a search committee should ask before retaining a consultant is, "Is this the person to whom we should transfer the image, reputation, and integrity of our ministry, even for a short time?" A selection committee may decide to engage

a consultant whose role is limited to presenting a process, coaching the committee on its application, and making sure the program stays on track. To choose a process consultant assumes that the committee chair is experienced in executive search with the time and energy to follow-up on nominations and personal contact with candidates. Committee members, as well, must be committed to accept working assignments from the chair for developing the list of candidates, making personal contacts, checking references, and being available for on-site visits. The merit of a process consultant guiding a working board is the sense of ownership and oneness that comes with such a commitment.

The main caution is to avoid a consultant who has a cookie-cutter approach to the process, misses the spiritual dynamics of the organization, floods the system with non-selective candidates, brags about past exploits or makes the search a personal conquest. A consultant who is a teacher as well as a recruiter and has a record for spiritual sensitivity as well as professional success will be an invaluable asset in the complicated process of the CEO search.

Charge to the Search Assistant

Every search committee needs an assistant who is committed to Jesus Christ, highly skilled in administrative matters and personal communication. This individual may well serve as the first contact with prospects by phone, email, and letter, the search assistant must have professional expertise in organizing an office, setting up systems, and managing the process. As the pivotal point for confidential information, the search assistant must have a track record of dealing with delicate information. Prompt responses to inquiries and a gracious but professional tone in phone, letter or email make this role a ministry in itself. Putting these tasks together, then, the charge to the search assistant is *to organize and manage the search office in support of the chair and the committee with professional skills and personal gifts in confidential communication reflecting the spirit of the organization.*

With the acceptance of these solemn charges by the board, board chair, search chair, search committee members, search assistant, and search consultant, the team is now in place and ready to function. No small task is ahead, but with the personal commitment of every participant to see the CEO search as a special calling to be a steward of a sacred trust, we go forward with confidence.

With All Due Diligence
Board Check
Sharing the Trust

As a show of full confidence in the integrity of relationships in our Christ-centered organization, our board has delegated responsibility for the search process to its representatives according to the following charges:

	Yes	No
1. The board is charged to:		
a. appoint the search chair	_____	_____
b. compose the search committee	_____	_____
c. approve the search plan	_____	_____
d. authorize outside consultation	_____	_____
e. order a search budget	_____	_____
f. set a search time schedule	_____	_____
2. The board chair is charged to:		
a. serve ex officio to the search committee	_____	_____
b. advise the search committee	_____	_____
c. communicate with key candidates	_____	_____
d. negotiate with finalists	_____	_____
3. The search chair is charged to:		
a. preside at search committee meetings	_____	_____
b. assure the integrity and confidentiality of the process	_____	_____

c. supervise the search assistant _____ _____

d. communicate with staff and public _____ _____

e. initiate key contacts _____ _____

f. mediate conflicts _____ _____

g. conduct interviews _____ _____

h. guide the committee to decision _____ _____

i. present the final recommendation to the board _____ _____

j. prepare a review and evaluation of search proceedings for history and future searches _____ _____

4. The search committee members are charged to:

a. attend all meetings _____ _____

b. sign the pledge of confidentiality _____ _____

c. represent his/her constituency _____ _____

d. rate the candidates according to Profile _____ _____

e. participate in the interviews _____ _____

f. seek the mind of God for the final decision _____ _____

5. The search consultant is charged to:

a. identify with the mission and spirit of the organization _____ _____

b. have sensitivity for the history, theology, culture, and strategic goals of the organization _____ _____

c. connect relationally with the
search chair and members of
the search committee   _____   _____

d. present a customized search process
based upon the distinctive character
of the ministry   _____   _____

e. take a selective approach to the
search based on quality rather
than breadth or numbers   _____   _____

f. participate in cost-effective
budgeting consistent with the
principles of Christian stewardship   _____   _____

g. Accept in-depth questions and
reference checks on past
performance in executive search   _____   _____

h. Represent the image and integrity
of the ministry in all contacts   _____   _____

6. The search assistant is charged to:

a. organize and manage the search office   _____   _____

b. report to the search chair   _____   _____

c. maintain search files, records and
minutes   _____   _____

d. arrange for meetings and interviews   _____   _____

e. compile ratings for candidates   _____   _____

f. communicate with candidates
as instructed   _____   _____

g. maintain confidentiality,
professionalism, and sensitivity
through the process.   _____   _____

Chapter 6

Overseeing CEO Selection
Profiling the Leader

The Leadership Profile is the keystone for the search. It assures not only the integrity and objectivity of the process itself but also reflects the distinctive mission and spirit of the Christ-centered organization. Boilerplate job descriptions borrowed from other organizations, from the Internet or from previous CEO searches by the organization violate these principles. Each organization has specific needs, unique to itself. Before the search can begin, the board must be dedicated to an in-depth study to affirm the convictions, prioritize the plans, and project the needs of the future. In this way a customized approach produces a Leadership Profile unique to the organization itself.

Affirming Our Identity

CEO transition is the time when the board needs to step back and affirm its foundational convictions, strategic priorities and leadership expectations. At a board retreat dedicated to this purpose, the agenda would include the review, discussion, revision and affirmation of these items:

1. Historical commitments

2. Theological convictions

3. Missional philosophy

4. Strategic goals—current and emerging priorities

5. Current CEO task description

As preparation for the board meeting, a knowledgeable board member can be assigned to review and present a brief paper on each of these items. A summary of affirmations at the end of each chapter will help focus the discussion on critical aspects of each area that needs to be considered foundational for the CEO search. After discussion, the board should officially adopt the affirmations as touchstones and the search committee will use them to write the Leadership Profile. The affirmations should also be circulated to staff.

Historical commitments. The phrase "community of memory," used by Sociologist Robert Bellah, refers to a history that is remembered, shared, and respected. This memory shapes an organization's character. The story unfolds in the biographies of leaders, the markers of change, and the turning points of policies. In a post-modern age, a Christ-centered organization needs to honor that memory without letting it become a deterrent to change. During CEO transition, the board serves best when it reflects on the memory that has shaped the past, imprints the present, and influences the future.

Theological convictions. By its very name, a Christ-centered, faith-based organization holds beliefs that are biblically grounded, theologically defined, and practically implemented. When these distinctions are lost, defection from the faith along a slippery slope is well documented in the history of Christian organizations. The YMCA and YWCA, for instance, were founded out of spiritual awakening in the 19th century but retain "Christian" in their names for historical purposes. For good reason, a board is fulfilling its trust when it uses the time of CEO transition to affirm its theological convictions.

Missional philosophy. Shifts in missional philosophy are as slippery as theological convictions. In the thrust for competitive marketing power, some Christ-centered organizations have made radical shifts in missional philosophy to qualify for government funding, competitive marketing and public acceptance. In such cases, it is the board that is ultimately accountable. Before searching for its next leader, the board must have a clear sense of the missional philosophy that it intends to pursue in the next generation.

Strategic priorities. Long-term planning with strategic goals, tactical decisions, and performance objectives is a credit to Christ-centered organizations. These plans, however, are not static. They must have the flexibility for push and pull with changing circumstances, internal and external. Their goals must be realistic and not set so far into the future that they create false expectations. At the time of CEO transition, the board will want to sit down, cast a discerning eye on the expectations, and pull back long-term plans into a manageable time frame. Generally speaking, a five-year period is good for setting expectations for CEO leadership. It also coincides with the average tenure of CEOs or for the time required to put new programs into place. These five-year priorities become touch points for screening and selecting CEO candidates. It is up to the board to establish these priorities and communicate the expectations to the search committee.

Leadership Profile. A CEO profile describes the character, skills, experience and educational background desired. If a consultant is used, the Leadership Profile is often drafted by the consultant in concert with the search committee for the board's approval. If a consultant is not used, the board must prepare its own Leadership Profile for board approval.

There may be a temptation to simply modify one of the organization's old Leadership Profiles. A dynamic organization changes over time. Preparing a fresh CEO profile with the future in mind is vital.

Constituent Survey

As a complement to the work of the board, a survey of selected constituents may have special value for the search process. People who are investing their lives and their money in the organization need to have a voice in setting the expectations and priorities for CEO leadership. Stakeholders within the organization, in particular, need what is often called a "sense of ownership" by an invitation to nominate candidates and participate in the survey. Inviting constituents to be involved shows trust, the glue for the community of faith.

The constituent survey also explains the search process. Rather than distributing a survey that is open-ended, responses can be guided by four questions:

1. What is your vision for the top three *strategic goals* to be achieved by the organization in the next five years (in order of priority)?

2. What are the top three *professional qualifications* needed for the new CEO to meet these goals (in order of priority)?

3. What are the top three *personal qualifications* for the new CEO as a complement to these professional qualifications (in order of priority)?

4. What are the top three affirmations of *spiritual maturity* you expect in a CEO candidate (in order of priority)?

Let the identity of the respondent be optional. Provide the results of the survey along with the Leadership Profile when it is completed. By limiting the questions to strategic goals, professional qualifications and personal qualifications, the survey keeps the focus upon expectations that will appear in the Profile. Most important, the respondents should be able to see the imprint of their collective thoughts in the final copy of the Profile.

Character, Competence, and Spirituality

Qualifications for CEO leadership in Christ-centered organizations differ from their secular counterparts in three essential ways.

First, *character is the entry point for CEO candidacy in a Christ-centered organization.* In recent years, secular organizations have given more credence to personal integrity and ethical character in their search process, but professional competence is still the starting point. Unless the private life of the candidate is smeared by criminal action or public scandal, it is not assumed to interfere with executive qualifications.

The secular world uses a "giving-getting" contract; the individual gives in proportion what he or she gets. The "giving" side is competence and the "getting" side is compensation. At best, the organization gets only pieces of the person. Even visionary and passionate CEOs who are personally identified as the face of the organization may have aspects of their private life that are considered irrelevant to executive competence.

In contrast, qualifications for the CEO of a Christ-centered organization invariably and unequivocally begin with the total person, so committed to Jesus Christ that His mind and spirit pervades the whole of life, including the workplace. This is not to say that character overrides competency. Incompetence at the executive level in Christian leadership is a waste of sacrificial resources, a blight on effective ministry, a disgrace before a watching world.

Gently, but firmly, then, candidates for CEO leadership are asked questions about character that range from ethical integrity in professional relationships to moral purity in personal relationships. Reference checking becomes a trust-and-verify process that probes the key questions and asks for examples. These give the search committee an in-depth picture of the character of the candidate. "Does the candidate have ethical integrity in all past professional relationships?" and "Does the candidate have moral integrity in all personal relationships?" When these questions are asked, astute reference checkers can discern any hesitations or reservations in the responses. Yellow flags require further explorations into character issues.

Second, *competence for CEOs for Christ-centered organizations is driven by responsibilities rather than results.* There is no mystery in the expectations for executive performance, whether in a secular or Christ-centered organization. In the 1950s, competencies were introduced under the acronym "POSDCORB"—Planning, Organizing, Staffing, Directing, Coordinating, Reporting and Budgeting. Over the years, these functions have been fleshed out in a variety of leadership styles that reflect the person as well as the task. Competency now includes vision for planning, strategy for organizing, teamwork for staffing, delegation for directing, collaboration for coordinating, feedback for reporting, and accountability for budgeting. All of these changes are positive, but the bottom line is that results are still the driving force for the secular model of executive leadership.

A CEO in an Christ-centered organization is not exempt from an assessment of performance based on results. But this cannot be the driving force. In the biblical model of leadership, Christ's disciples are only called to be obedient to the means of ministry and leave the results to the work of the Holy Spirit. Otherwise, we quickly fall to the temptation of hubris that comes with grasping for success and bragging about our results. Jesus' mandate in the Great Commission leaves no doubt. He commands us to "Go," "Make," "Baptize," and "Teach." Our only guarantee is His presence in the Holy Spirit—to Whom the harvest belongs. Therefore, when we talk about competencies for CEO leadership in Christ-centered organizations, we should think about calling related to vision, wisdom related to systems, purity related to motive, self-giving related to people, prayer related to power, conviction related to decisions, compassion related to conflict, sacrifice related to reconciliation, stewardship related to resources, and humility related to outcomes. These are virtues that move us toward the most significant difference in the criteria for CEO selection.

Third, *in the Christ-centered organization, CEO selection advances integrity of character to the evidence of the Spirit-filled life.* In the Acts of the Apostles, the qualifications for Christian leadership are simplified in the Profile for selecting the seven deacons of the early church. When controversy over limited resources calls out the need for executive leadership, the Apostles announce, *Brothers, chose seven men from among you who are known to be full of the Spirit and wisdom. We will turn this responsibility over to them and give our attention to prayer and the ministry of the Word* (Acts 6:34).

From this scripture, Phillips' transliteration sorts out three criteria for executive leadership: "a good reputation, practical wisdom, and a Spirit-filled life." What more do we need? A good reputation both inside and outside the church reveals character that has stood the test of public scrutiny. Practical wisdom is the competency to administer the details of an organization without losing sight of the big picture. A Spirit-filled life is the witness to the power and passion of a personal Pentecost seen in the fruit of the Spirit—"love, joy, peace, patience, kindness, goodness, and faithfulness, gentleness, and self-control" (Galatians 5:22-23).

Results now count. Hard evidence of the fruit of the Spirit in the practice of leadership is the witness for the Spirit-filled life. Is it too much to include the following questions in the formal application for the candidates self-assessment?

Do you, as a CEO candidate to lead our Christ-centered organization, demonstrate the fruit of the Spirit-filled life through:

1. **Love**—sacrificing self for the needs of others?
2. **Joy**—communicating a sense of inner gladness?
3. **Peace**—remaining poised under pressure?
4. **Patience**—moving fast, but never in a hurry?
5. **Kindness**—welcoming anyone and everyone with grace?
6. **Goodness**—acting without ulterior motives?
7. **Faithfulness**—making good every promise and every word?
8. **Gentleness**—handling authority and power with humility?
9. **Self-control**—disciplining natural impulses and desires?

In addition to serving as a guide for spiritual assessment by the candidate, *these questions are invaluable for checking with references who know the person,* especially when examples are given. If, then, the candidate is selected as CEO, these same questions become a guide for a growth plan that includes maturing spirituality.

Are we being intrusive if we ask these questions? I think not. More and more, Christ-centered organizations and their CEOs are dealing with internal matters of conflict and external matters of hostility which can make or break our witness. To assure the integrity of our divine commission, our biblical convictions, our sacrificial service, and our redemptive results, our boards depend on the character, competence, and spirituality of the CEO.

The Leadership Profile

With this wealth of information in hand, the search committee can draft a executive profile that will reflect the character of the organization, its goals for the future, and its priorities for leadership. A general outline would include the following sections:

1. **Preamble.** The board's invitation for applications from qualified individuals whose personal and professional traits point toward leadership in a Christ-centered organization.

2. **Strategic priorities.** A specific statement of current and projected organizational goals that infer key leadership expectations for the CEO.

3. **Professional qualifications.** A selective list of executive skills, experiences, and credentials essential to success in the position.

4. **Personal qualifications.** A complementary list of personal gifts, commitments and relationships that sets the tone for CEO leadership.

5. **Spiritual qualifications.** An extension of the qualifications of character and competency toward a biblically-based witness of maturing spirituality.

6. **Special information.** A statement of confidentiality, a commitment to Equal Employment Opportunity Commission (EEOC) requirements of nondiscrimination except for religion, and instructions for submitting the preliminary application.

After the search committee completes the draft in preparation for adoption by the board, a final step is to ask whether or not the Leadership Profile:

1. mirrors the historical, theological, and missional heritage of the ministry;

2. communicates the distinctive character of this ministry;

3. identifies the strategic goals for taking the ministry to the next level of effectiveness;

4. relates the strategic goals to the priorities for CEO leadership;

5. pre-selects prospects on such factors as evangelical theology, spiritual maturity, professional credentials, church membership, senior executive experience, and constituent relationships;

6. makes clear the expectations for age, sex, health, disability, family relationships, longevity in office, moral character, etc.;

7. implies the performance goals on which CEO leadership will be assessed;

8. coincides with any legal requirements for hiring practices;

9. translates into a score sheet of expectations for the screening of candidates and the selection of the CEO; and

10. instructs prospective candidates on the procedures for application.

If the Leadership Profile meets these tests and is approved by the search committee, it is ready for presentation to the board for final review and adoption. The approved copy is then circulated back to the staff and external constituency, posted on the CEO search website, and adapted for advertising and public relations functions. From now on, at every phase of the process, the Leadership Profile will be the checkpoint to assure the integrity and objectivity of search.

With All Due Diligence
Board Check
Profiling the Position

Is the Leadership Profile adopted by our board as the touchstone for the search process:

	Yes	No
1. grounded in the theological and historical heritage of our ministry?	_____	_____
2. centered in the mission statement of our ministry?	_____	_____
3. reflective of the distinctive character of our ministry?	_____	_____
3. consistent with the strategic plan for the ministry?	_____	_____
4. unequivocal on the priorities for CEO leadership?	_____	_____
5. effective in pre-screening prospects who do not qualify?	_____	_____
6. definitive on professional expectations for the CEO, e.g., executive experience, academic credentials, leadership style, etc.?	_____	_____
7. clear on personal expectations for the CEO, e.g., integrity, health, family, church activity, etc.?	_____	_____
8. affirmative on spiritual expectations, e.g., fullness and fruit of the Spirit?	_____	_____

9. specific on performance goals by which
   the CEO will be assessed?   _____   _____

10. written to assure compliance with
    relevant legal requirements?   _____   _____

11. instructive for the prospect who applies?   _____   _____

Chapter 7

Overseeing CEO Selection
Spreading a Selective Net

Boards are often caught off guard when a CEO resigns, retires or is dismissed. Rather than having a ready pool of prospects or someone who has been groomed for the position, we often have to begin at square one in identifying, contacting, and inviting candidates to consider the position. A premium is often placed upon having a large number of prospects from a national search. The numbers become "brag points" for the search committee or consultant. This is false economy for a Christ-centered organization because developing the prospect pool is a highly selective process. If the Leadership Profile is an effective tool for pre-screening prospects prior to application, the pool may be smaller but with greater potential for identifying qualified persons. Plus, significant dollars may be saved because every person who expresses active interest or submits an application deserves full and fair appraisal. A premium should be placed upon a selective sweep yielding a pre-screened number of highly-qualified candidates.

Spreading the Net

Ideally, the search process begins with a selective list of candidates already identified with the organization or who have been recognized for their leadership potential within the scope of the organization. Practically, however, the search process still requires the spread of a public and private net to make sure that all highly-qualified candidates are included.

The public net. Even though a CEO search is a highly selective process for Christ-centered organizations, information about the position and invitations for applicants go far and wide. This is in keeping with the public relations goal to use the search process as an opportunity to communicate the mission and vision of the organization to a variety of publics. In its widest sweep, ads are placed in periodicals or on websites that draw from non-selective sources.

For religious organizations, the organization should review the EEOC statement that accompanies the ad with professional counsel. There is an EEOC exception for religious organizations to give employment preference to members of their own religion. Therefore, if this exception applies to your organization you will likely want to state qualifiers in the ad. Not all religious organizations qualify for the EEOC exception. Thus, the determination of whether an organization is a religious organization under the EEOC may require legal counsel.

Ads often elicit applications from scores of unqualified persons. Many of them are simply desperate to be a CEO. If they apply, you are obligated to process their applications and become exposed to possible litigation from those who want to charge discrimination on such grounds as gender, age, or sexual preference. Experience tells us that advertising in non-selective journals is usually non-productive.

Ads in the Christian media (print and online) are often used to announce the search and to post the position with the evangelical community. These ads serve the public relations goal for positioning the organization in the Christian community. The results are usually limited and will often surface individuals who are professionals at applying for CEO positions. Although these publications lack the risks we noted earlier, they are a test of the Leadership Profile because of the historical, theological and educational distinctions among Christ-centered organizations. If the ad is generically "Christian" or "evangelical" and the search criteria are even less selective, it is patently unfair to invite applicants who will be rejected on hidden expectations.

Coming closer to home, the net is spread to cover members of the internal organization and relevant constituencies. A copy of the Leadership Profile and an invitation to nominate should be sent by letter, email or web posting to the board, administration, staff, donors, church, alumni, and other constituent leaders who have a stake in the organization. Expectations will be high from these sectors, but there is often disappointment. Sentimental favorites, marginally qualified hopefuls, and friends and family are often presented. Still, in comparison with the wider net, there is a good chance that promising prospects will come forward.

Pulling the net even tighter, more fruitful contacts come from the network connections of leaders of Christ-centered organizations. Led by the search consultant and the search chair, personal contacts making requests for nominations based on the Leadership Profile will surface the names of senior executives with CEO experience and junior executives with CEO potential. CEOs in the fraternity of Christ-centered ministries committed to growing their own people can be the most helpful. Still another source is the list of candidates from other CEO searches in the same or related field. (It is no shame to be rejected for a position when the emphasis is upon a Spirit-guided match for the individual and the organization.)

The board itself should be a primary source of nominations for CEO leadership. In a recent search, after all nominations were in, a board member felt prompted by the Holy Spirit to broach candidacy with an established vice president of a major university. Position, salary, and benefits seemed to put him out of range. But when approached with the idea, he was immediately interested. The same Spirit had been prompting him to consider a change that would take him to ministry in a Christ-centered organization. Board members intimately acquainted with the needs of their organization willing to step out guided by the Spirit are primary sources for CEO nominations.

From these sources in the public net, a fairly select pool of prospects can be developed. The emphasis should be upon quality rather than quantity because of the cost in time, energy and money in following these leads.

The private net. While all candidates for the CEO position must be considered according to the Leadership Profile, special provision should be made for prospects who will not apply through the public net and are in sensitive positions, such as sitting CEOs or senior executives of other Christ-centered organizations. These are proven leaders in the field and highly qualified as a match for the expectations in the Leadership Profile. They are not looking for a job. A search committee must ask the question, "Who is the best qualified candidate to be our CEO, bar none?" In answer, a short list will arise that often includes sitting CEOs of other educational, religious, corporate or governmental organizations. Sensitivity to the situation will determine who should make a personal contact— the board chair, search chair, search consultant or a search committee member. With the assurance of full confidence and the willingness to honor the prospect's time schedule, these contacts will produce pleasant surprises as well as ready rejections. Timing is the key for putting them into the private net. In most cases, they will have to be nurtured into candidacy through close personal communication. If interest continues, negotiation may be required to decide when the prospect officially becomes a candidate and enters the search process. Usually it will be after the prospects in the public net have gone through initial screening. Sooner or later, however, the private net prospect must declare active interest in the position and clear the lines of communication with superiors in his or her own organization. As delicate as it seems, a search committee should not just sit back and wait for candidates to come. If there is confidence in the opportunity presented by our ministry, we will go enthusiastically to the best prospects and say, "We want you!"

The Internal Candidate

Internal candidates pose a special challenge to the search committee. No one should be blocked out of the search due to employment within the organization. Everyone is open to become a candidate for the CEO position.

An internal candidate comes to the search with both an advantage and a handicap. The advantage is that the person knows the organization and is known by the members of the search committee. At the same time, this advantage has the handicap of highly personalized judgments about the person's qualifications for the position. The search committee needs high level diplomacy when the individual is a mismatch for the position. Even higher level diplomacy is needed when the individual is a favorite son or daughter of the constituency.

In one of my first stints as a board member of a Christ-centered organization, the search committee presented two names for the CEO position. One was a well-known insider; the other was a newly introduced outsider. Debate in the board roared on for more than four hours. Vote after vote produced no majority. As the conversation deteriorated, opponents of the insider began to pick away at minor flaws while advocates of the outsider countered by noting their candidate was strong in the area of the insider's weakness. Finally, the vote turned on the fact that the outsider was strong in remembering the names of the board members after the introduction. In one swoop, he was elected as the "people person" needed by the organization. Two years later, he was dismissed for the failure to make tough decisions.

This kind of horror story need not be. In another CEO search, there were three finalists. One was the second in command of the organization. His inside knowledge gave him an edge, but the other two finalists had compensating qualities that balanced out the final ticket. The search committee labored for two days. They brought back the candidates for second interviews before concluding that the inside candidate's vision for the future was the deciding factor. When his name was presented to the board, the search chair meticulously traced the process that led to his election. Twenty years later, he still leads and serves with great distinction.

Here again, clarity of expectations in the Leadership Profile and the rigor of the search process came to the rescue. Internal prospects who do not meet the expectations should be graciously dismissed by the search chair rather than being carried along because of sentiment. Likewise, favorite sons or daughters should be scrutinized with the same requirements in application, reference checking, and interviews as external candidates. Emotions and personal preferences must be put aside in order to fairly assess the individual on objective criteria. In fact, the search chair should ask committee members if their perceptions are coloring the chances of the candidate one way or the other. On more than one occasion, when an organization has a proven leader who is ready for chief executive leadership, I have recommended against the bragging rights of an open, national search and said to the board chair, "Work the process and if the individual comes through, make the appointment."

The question is always asked, "Can the interim CEO be a candidate for the permanent position?" Experience weighs heavily against such a possibility because incumbency has advantages that distort the fairness of the search process and cause top prospects, especially sitting CEOs, to shy away from application because of the risk involved. In one case, a very successful sitting CEO accepted candidacy for the CEO of a prominent Christian ministry in another part of the country. He became a finalist along with the interim CEO for the organization. When his turn came to interview with the board, he quickly perceived that he was the straw man in the process. The interim CEO had been careful to keep his head down and his mouth shut during the months of the search process while the retiring leader lobbied on his behalf with key members of the board. Consequently, the sitting CEO's interview was a formality with a foregone conclusion. The man held his anger but left disillusioned; he had risked his present position to be a candidate.

Given our options, then, it is generally best that the board set the requirement that the interim CEO not be a candidate for the permanent position. If the exiting CEO has met the responsibility to cultivate emerging leaders within the organization, there may be more than one person capable of serving in the interim role.

The Preliminary Application

Any prospect who shows interest is invited to respond by submitting four items of personal information: (a) *Letter of Interest* based upon qualifications that match the Leadership Profile; (b) *Statement of Faith* consistent with the organizations' position; (c) *Personal and Professional Resume*; and six *References*, three from professional colleagues and three from personal friends, including the applicant's pastor. The search chair or search assistant immediately acknowledges receipt of the application.

A preliminary score sheet based upon the essentials of the Leadership Profile gives a quick reading on the qualifications of the prospects. The score sheet includes a rating of the match between organizational priorities and individual gifts, compatibility of faith position, professional qualifications for chief executive leadership, and personal qualifications for the role as revealed in the resume. The search chair has the first look at the preliminary applications and has the prerogative of writing a letter of rejection if there are obvious factors that would disqualify the applicant. Such action would be reported to the search committee and confirmed in the official minutes.

As a result of the review of the preliminary applications, the search committee decides either to invite the qualified prospects to proceed with a formal application or indicate that the applicant is not being advanced. The phone call or letter of rejection should never reveal the reason for the decision. A prompt and gracious "Thank you" for the time and energy taken to apply along with a request for prayer as the process goes forward will keep the prospect as a friend of the ministry.

Although it is preferable that the prospect pool be complete before the initial cut is made, an argument can be made for some flexibility on announced deadlines. If a highly qualified candidate comes into the search after the initial cut or even later, there would be no advantage or disadvantage because all candidates are judged by the same criteria in the Leadership Profile. However, such cases should be the exception rather than the rule.

With the development of the prospect pool and the initial screening, each person invited to make formal application will be one of whom the search committee believes, "This person could be our CEO." The task is to narrow the field to a limited number of semi-finalists whose candidacy is explored in depth through personal conversation, reference checks, site visits, and formal interviews.

With All Due Diligence
Board Check
Spreading the Selective Net

In the initial step of developing a pool of prospects for the position of CEO, has the search committee addressed these questions:

	Yes	No
1. Have we decided how selective we want our search to be?	____	____
2. Have we identified the constituencies, publics and networks from which to develop our pool of prospects?	____	____
3. Have we developed a plan to announce the position to these constituencies, publics or networks?	____	____
4. Are our ads or announcements pre-screening the prospects?	____	____
5. Have we set target numbers for each stage in the process?	____	____
6. Are non-qualified applicants graciously rejected?	____	____
7. Does the preliminary application include:		
a. Letter of interest,	____	____
b. Statement of faith,	____	____
c. Resume,	____	____
d. Six preliminary references.	____	____

8. Are all of these included in the packet of information sent to prospects:

a. Search chair's letter? _____ _____

b. Leadership Profile? _____ _____

c. Organizational profile? _____ _____

d. Statement of faith? _____ _____

9. Is the search committee leaning primarily upon the search consultant for developing the pool? _____ _____

10. Has a private net of top candidates currently in positions been developed? _____ _____

11. Are the board chair and search chair engaged in sensitive and confidential conversations with key contacts? _____ _____

12. Are internal or "favorite" candidates treated with the same rigor and objectivity of other candidates? _____ _____

13. Has the search committee taken ownership of the process by attendance, ratings, discussion and decisions? _____ _____

14. Do the ratings sheets based on the Leadership Profile give the objectivity needed for full discussion and fair decisions? _____ _____

15. Are search committee decisions communicated immediately to the applicants? _____ _____

16. Does the pool of candidates advanced for further consideration represent a manageable number of highly qualified candidates? _____ _____

Chapter 8

Overseeing CEO Selection Screening for Quality

Alfter the initial screening of the prospect pool is complete, the advanced stage of selecting candidates who qualify as semi-finalists begins. Although there are no magic numbers for each stage of the process, the aim is to make the work manageable and more selective as the candidates advance. In the search for a Christ-centered organization, a pool of 40-50 prospects who complete the preliminary application is a very heavy workload. Perhaps half that number will be invited to complete the formal application with its implications for in-depth work by the search committee and the search consultant. The next step is to narrow the field to five to eight semi-finalists for the critical stage of preliminary interviews, reference checking and on-site visits.

The Formal Application

The formal application is a mirror image of the Leadership Profile. Its priorities, qualifications and expectations are now translated into probing questions for the candidate. Primary selectors such as understanding the mission, sharing the vision, and embracing the statement of faith are first-cut criteria for screening applicants. Strategic priorities follow. The applicant's response may not be as precise as the stated goals, but there must be a strong connection between the candidate's gifts and those goals. For example, if a capital campaign is on the horizon, candidates should respond to that priority with energy, experience and success.

If CEO experience is an expectation, it should be high on the list and weighted accordingly on score sheets. Personal qualifications are more delicate. Evidence of spiritual maturity, family relationships, servant spirit, church participation, and other personal qualities are better explored in personal interviews where the nuances of body language, facial expression, and tone of voice are often key. Legal issues require that age, sex, race and disability must be respected. Direct questions in these areas cannot be asked.

Applications usually include queries about the candidate being convicted of a crime, dismissed from a job or under psychiatric treatment. Now it is also appropriate to ask, "Is there anything in your background, if revealed, would be an embarrassment to you or the organization?" If the answer is "Yes," the search committee can decide whether to explore it further or reject the applicant. At the end of the application, the committee should state that it reserves the right to check unsolicited references named by solicited references when asked, "Is there anyone else whom you recommend that we contact?" It may be the unsolicited reference who provides the most critical information.

Although the formal application is an onerous task for the candidates, it tests the seriousness of their intent. Are they willing to go beyond the textbook examples of leadership to cite examples from their own experience? Are they willing to deal with sensitive factors? Are they willing to admit that there are areas where they need growth? Are they willing to open the door to additional references? Are they willing to let the search committee or the search consultant follow references other than those the candidate named? The formal application is an invitation for the probe to go deeper.

Rating the Application

When members of the search committee review the formal applications, it is often helpful to work from a rating sheet with weighted factors, numerical scores on items and provision for comments and questions. After rating sheets are complete, the results are reported at the committee meeting. To narrow the number of semi-finalists, formal decisions recorded in the minutes are made to accept, reject or hold each applicant. If put in the "hold" category, further information is needed to make a full and fair decision. Again, the test is not to advance a certain number as semi-finalists but to be sure that each of them truly has the potential to be CEO.

Introducing the Private Net

At this time, candidates from the private net are introduced. Timing may be critical for their organization's fiscal year, annual meeting date, or academic year. For candidates who are incumbent CEOs, a reasonable amount of time is needed to prepare for the possibility of change. In most cases, a sitting CEO is expected to notify his or her current board chair of a conversation with the search committee. Because the initiative would have come from the search committee, the incumbent CEO can report that fact while honestly stating that a show of interest kept the conversation going. Successful CEOs often receive inquires about other positions, so this confidential conversation between the private net prospect and the board chair should not jeopardize the executive's current status. The key is for the prospect to be fully open and up-to-date with both board chairs.

Selecting the Candidate

Intensity takes over when the committee explores the leadership potential of the semi-finalists in depth, now including willing prospects from the private net.

Immediately after the meeting when the semi-finalists are selected, the search chair notifies the applicants by phone and follows with a letter. No information is given except the decision of the committee and generous thanks for willingness to complete the formal application and go through the process.

Reference checks. Not enough can be said about the importance of reference checks. Early on, we learned that you can never go deep enough to reduce the unknowns about the candidate. Steve Ballmer, president of Microsoft, advises, "Ask enough and ask around." In one Christ-centered organization, an outstanding candidate was selected to be the nominee for the presidency. Just before being presented to the board, a belated reference check came in from a university where the candidate claimed an advanced degree. The transcript revealed that he had attended classes but never graduated. Because of this breach of integrity, he was dismissed. Ironically, the person elected president did not have an advanced degree either. If the first man had been honest, he would have had the position.

A consultant who excels in the field of reference checking brings a special advantage to this kind of inquiry. In addition to knowing which questions to ask and when to probe further, the consultant is able to compare all of the candidates in the semi-finalist pool. A strong case can also be made for reference checking by the search committee itself. If provided with a reference checking form that mirrors the Leadership Profile in its questions and coached by the consultant on the do's and don'ts, their investment enriches committee discussions as they make their report. Given the choice, involving committee members, with the consultant coaching and spot-checking, is preferred as an effective tool and learning experience.

Phone interviews and on-site visits. The review of applications will always result in questions that need follow-up. Rather than starting personal interviews, which are costly at this stage of the process, the search chair, committee members or the consultant can conduct a focused phone interview with a candidate. On occasion a conference call with the search committee can also be used. In either instance, the conversation should be limited to the questions that need to be answered or issues that need clarification.

On-site visits with the candidate by the board chair, search chair, committee member or search team have the value of seeing the candidate on his or her home turf. With a sharp eye out for the way the candidate is perceived among peers or in family relationships, the on-site visit adds a dimension that cannot be matched by interviews on a neutral site or away from home.

Selecting the finalists. Once full information on the semi-finalists is in, the search committee is ready to make its choice of finalists. If the process has been effective to this point, the priorities of the Leadership Profile have sorted out the candidates on comparative strengths and weaknesses. Now, as the search narrows and the candidates come closer together, it is more and more difficult for the committee to choose the limited number, perhaps three, who will be finalists.

At this point, the key question is, "Which of the candidates are best qualified to serve as our CEO according to the criteria of the Leadership Profile?" The committee must advance only those persons who are fully qualified and ready for executive leadership. To be "fully qualified" means that the person could effectively serve as CEO. A cardinal sin of CEO searches is to select finalists just for the sake of numbers or to send forward a straw man who does not have a chance of being selected. The search committee puts its integrity on the line when it chooses finalists, any one of whom they might recommend to the board. The task is to choose the best among the best.

With All Due Diligence
Board Check
Screening for Quality

After screening the pool of prospects down to a selective list of viable candidates who will be invited to advance in the process, the search committee will stop to check whether or not the following questions have been asked:

	Yes	No
1. What is the manageable number to be advanced to semi-finalist interviews?	_____	_____
2. How do we choose the best among the best of the candidates?	_____	_____
3. Are the priorities in the Leadership Profile being emphasized?	_____	_____
4. Is the Leadership Profile reflected in these selection materials:		
a. Formal application,	_____	_____
b. Reference checking form,	_____	_____
c. Follow up calls and/or visits,	_____	_____
d. Rating forms,	_____	_____
e. Search Committee agenda?	_____	_____
5. What priority for leadership comes through as most important of all?	_____	_____
6. What are deal breakers for rejecting candidates?	_____	_____

7. Are references checked in depth, including those who may not have been on the candidates' list? _____ _____

8. Are private net candidates now in the process? _____ _____

9. Are candidates who are advanced to interviews:

   a. best-qualified among the qualified? _____ _____

   b. best matched to the Leadership Profile? _____ _____

   c. committed to accept the position if offered? _____ _____

   d. cleared on questions of character and health? _____ _____

10. Are the candidates immediately and graciously notified of the decision, whether advanced, rejected, or put on hold, without further explanation? _____ _____

Chapter 9

Overseeing CEO Selection
Making the Match

In the final step for selecting one candidate to present to the board, confidentiality, timing and intensity drive the process. Increased confidentiality protects the finalists from premature judgments outside of the search committee. The pace is sped up to shorten the periods between the steps and therefore reduce the opportunity for mischief or manipulation. Intensity deepens as the search committee delves into the details of personal interviews and the delicacies of site visits. In the highly selective process of CEO search, we are rapidly coming to the point when a refined instrument is ready for presentation.

Critical Steps

A common commitment. When a finalist is notified of the decision by the search committee, the commitments of both parties are clear. The search chair can report that a select number of persons has been chosen, any one of whom is qualified to serve as CEO. Moreover, it is fair for the search chair to ask the candidate, "On the basis of what you know now, are you willing to serve if elected?" The candidate may still have questions that can only be answered by personal interviews and campus visits, but the committee must know whether he or she has a commitment keeping pace with the search committee's decisions.

Advanced reference checks. Reference checking continues into the finalist stage. By now, it is assumed that the references given by the candidate have been checked. In concluding these phone interviews, two common questions should be asked: (a) "Is there anything that I have not asked that I should have asked?" and (b) "Is there anyone else whom you suggest that I might call about the candidate?" This latter question is very delicate, but also very revealing. Names are given that did not appear on the list submitted by the candidate, and more often than not, these are people who have a deeper insight into the character of the candidate or into sensitive issues. In the formal application, the candidate has agreed that the search committee reserved the right to check references other than those given as part of the process. Some candidates may ask to be informed of such calls, but the committee must be able to make them to assure a thorough search.

Professional tests. The opinions of search committees vary widely about professional tests, such as medical examinations and personality profiles. If they are to be included in the process, they should be agreed to in the formal application. Tests should be chosen for an intended purpose. A variety of self-administered tests may be used to profile personality characteristics or identify leadership gifts and abilities. In rare cases, the search committee may request and fund the cost of a test such as the California Psychological Inventory given by a licensed psychologist.

There is a natural hesitancy to go beyond reference checking and the personal interview. In one search, however, a president who passed through the reference checks and finalist interview with flying colors failed miserable within months after assuming the position. A professional psychological inventory might have revealed the character flaws that led to failure.

Finalist Interview

Everything in the search process comes to a focus in the finalist interviews. With the Leadership Profile more dominant than ever, the candidates and spouses (if applicable) agree to a personal conversation upon which the final decision of the committee will turn.

The interview schedule itself must be paced for maximum effectiveness. Three hours should be allotted to each candidate with a break mid-way through the session. The search chair is the facilitator and committee members are fully briefed on the part they will play. The key is to stay on schedule without having the interview appear stilted. The following schedule illustrates good pacing:

1. Welcome and prayer—Search Chair

2. Introduction of the candidate—Search Chair

3. Preliminary statements, such as "My/Our Spiritual Journey"—candidate and spouse, if applicable

4. Core questions—Search committee members

5. Customized questions for candidate—Search committee members

6. Break

7. Customized questions continued—Search committee members

8. Candidate's questions for the committee—CEO candidate and spouse, if applicable

9. Summary and final questions—Search chair

10. Closing communal prayer—Search chair

Key elements in the schedule include providing for a preliminary statement by the candidate (and spouse, if applicable). An invitation to speak for five to eight minutes each about their spiritual journey lets them warm up for the questions to follow and gives the committee a feeling for their spiritual maturity to go along with their statement of faith. The core questions then become the centerpiece for the interview because the same questions will be asked of each candidate and ranked for comparison in the committee's final deliberations. Just as the questions in the formal application sought out evidence of experience and examples to support written answers, the core questions in the interview will focus upon critical issues and how the candidates would handle them as CEO. The issues may be framed out of real or projected circumstances in the organization. Examples of critical issues might include:

1. You are elected CEO by a board that has been known to blur the lines between policy and execution by micromanaging from time to time. How will you work with the board on issues of governance?

2. An economic downturn causes a serious reduction in gifts for your ministry. How will you make adjustments in budget related to people and programs to cope with this new reality?

3. Your vision as CEO involves a major shift in priorities for the ministry of your organization. How will you go about preparing the organization for change and implementing your vision?

4. A long-time employee has challenged the "evangelical" identity of your Christ-centered ministry and is gathering internal support for his position. As CEO, how will you address this challenge?

5. Confidential word comes to you about a man and woman on your staff, both married with families, who are the subject of rumors because of indiscrete behavior. How will you handle the situation?

6. A donor offers you a multi-million dollar gift with the condition that he be named a member of the board. What will be your response?

7. You inherit a vice president who is deeply spiritual and widely loved, but a performance review shows that he is

woefully ineffective and resists accountability. How will you work with him?

8. You are elected as CEO with the expectation that you will lead a major capital campaign. How will you go about this task?

9. You are interviewing a candidate for the position of second-in-command and the one who will lead in your absence. What are the three top questions that you would want to ask?

10. A strategic plan gathers dust in the closet. How will you restart the planning process and what will be the role of the board, your executive team, and professional staff?

Between the lines of questions like these, a search committee will be able to read the candidate's views on governing, leading, planning, budgeting, decision-making, hiring, and firing as well as issues that are theological and spiritual in nature. Real-life critical incidents involving moral conflict and requiring a hard decision will reveal the most about a candidate. Even more important is to ask for examples from experience. It is one thing to frame hypothetical questions and quite another thing to learn whether or not the candidate has actually dealt with similar issues.

Following the core questions, the search committee should focus its attention on the customized questions for the individual candidate. These may relate to inquiries about competence or character that have been in the minds of the committee. As difficult as it may be, if there is an "elephant in the room," it must be confronted.

In fairness to the candidate, sufficient time must be allowed in the three-hour session for the individual to ask questions of the committee. Particular attention should be given to the kind of questions asked. Experienced executives will often spot gaps in the Leadership Profile that reveal the depth of their understanding. One candidate, for instance, saw a figure in the annual audit that even the board had missed. Another asked about the travel expectations for the CEO, an item that had not been discussed. If the candidate is married, the spouse should be invited to ask questions as well. All antennas are up for clues that may predict whether or not the finalist will remain a viable candidate. In almost every search, there is an instance in which the spouse vetoes the candidacy. The reluctance to move homes, change schools for the children, leave parents, give up careers, transfer positions or feel compatible with the new culture are all legitimate concerns that can make a difference. For this reason, provision is made for the spouse to speak at the beginning of the interview, answer questions in the process, and ask questions at the end. When the search chair asks the candidate, "If elected, will you serve?" the answer may well be in the eyes of the spouse.

An interview is not without its taboos. For one, the candidate should not be allowed to take over the interview. In one case, a finalist stopped the search chair while being introduced to the committee to say, "May I ask a question?" Out of courtesy the chair answered, "Yes," but when one question led to another, it took a full hour to get the interview back on track.

Another taboo is against whining. Candidates who resort to boss-bashing, blame-casting and name dropping are instantly suspect because such antics persist as a flaw in character and a weakness in leadership. If they whine about the past, they will whine about the future.

Still another taboo is against a discussion of contractual negotiations. This is the responsibility of the board chair in private conversation immediately after the interview, and the candidate should be informed of this timing before the interview begins. Although the search chair may provide general information about the CEO's package (such as citing ranges in the percentiles for compensation from surveys conducted by ECFA or the Council for Christian Colleges & Universities, for example), the details for negotiation belong in a meeting between the board chair and the finalist and at the close of that conversation about the chief executive's package, the board chair should again ask, "If elected, will you serve?"

The Selection Session

After each finalist has been interviewed, the search committee members should closet themselves to rate the candidate on the core questions and make notes on other responses that will help in the final session. The search assistant compiles the results on the core questions and note any common concerns of the members that arise from the customized questions. Reporting these results will help focus the agenda for the search committee as it begins the decision of selection.

Again, timing is crucial for the final meeting of the search committee. A long lapse between the finalist interviews and the selection of the candidate invites mischief. This is particularly true when the finalists are involved in a site visit and staff and constituent groups form diverse opinions. Even though none of these groups can vote, the internal dynamics of internal communication and politics will come into play. In one case, faculty members took advantage of the lag time by calling colleagues at the organization where the candidate served as president, circulating a negative report, and squashing the candidacy. If the meeting to select the final candidate had immediately followed the interviews, this travesty might have been avoided.

The Decisive Vote

After a thorough discussion comparing the finalists' rankings, the time has come for a vote. Prior to a vote, the committee would have decided how much of a majority would be required. The search chair calls for a vote by secret ballot. If there is a tie, the search chair casts the deciding vote. When the majority is achieved, the candidate is selected. At that time, a motion is in order to cast a unanimous ballot in favor of the selectee. Any member who does not favor the vote by acclamation still has the privilege of having a negative or abstaining vote recorded in the search committee's minutes.

With the spiritual goal of seeing the will of God done and fervent prayer guiding each step, it is memorable to witness the blending of diverse minds and spirits into a unanimous decision. It may not happen every time, but it is worthy goal for which all can pray. A search committee that can celebrate that outcome has the strongest case for presenting the recommendation of its future leader to the board.

With All Due Diligence
Board Check
Making the Match

As our board comes to the crucial time of selecting the best among the best of finalists for the CEO position, special attention is given to these questions:

	Yes	No
1. Is full confidentiality still held?	_____	_____
2. Is timing picking up speed?	_____	_____
3. Is the search committee fully committed to the candidate?	_____	_____
4. Is the candidate fully committed to the position as CEO?	_____	_____
5. Have advanced references been checked?	_____	_____
6. Have psychological tests been used?	_____	_____
7. Has the interview been planned to be efficient and gracious?	_____	_____
8. Is the interview conducted professionally under the guidance of the Spirit?	_____	_____
9. Are ratings of the interviews compiled for committee discussion prior to decision?	_____	_____
10. Is post-interview time allotted for the board chair to meet the candidate, discuss terms, and initiate a relationship?	_____	_____

11. Are candidates invited to meet with
    staff or constituents without violating
    the board's sole authority to elect
    the CEO?   _____   _____

12. Is the selection of the candidate
    done by secret ballot?   _____   _____

13. Before a vote, has a decision been made
    as to how much of a majority will be
    required (i.e., simple majority, super
    majority, etc.).   _____   _____

14. Was a unanimous ballot cast to show
    the unity of the selection committee?   _____   _____

Chapter 10

Overseeing CEO Selection
Electing God's Choice

All of the long hours of exhausting and sometimes frustrating work of the search committee are rewarded when the candidate is presented to the board for election. The search chair, who has led the committee through the arduous process, has the privilege of making the presentation.

Agenda for the Board Meeting

Whether the election of the CEO takes place at a regular or special session of the board, the item must stand out as the single most important matter on the agenda. After the call to order with devotions and prayer, the board chair calls upon the search chair to present the candidate. The search chair begins by reviewing the process to remind the board members of its rigor and tie it directly to the Leadership Profile as the touchstone for screening and selecting a candidate. Building on this background, the search chair reports the recommendation of the search committee and presents the candidate as the person who has emerged as best-qualified among all candidates to assume chief executive leadership. If portions of the finalist interviews were taped, the board profits from seeing a clip of the candidate (and spouse, if applicable) in an interactive setting. After the search chair's presentation, it is time to convene the board in executive session so that the members will feel free to ask any questions about the process or persons who may have been candidates.

Once the board members are clear on the process leading to the recommendation, the search chair invites the candidate (and spouse) into the meeting for a formal introduction. The professional qualifications are already well known, so the search chair can emphasize the relational bond that has developed between candidate and committee in common commitment to seek God's will in its decision. This gives the candidate the platform from which to make a statement to the board about his or her vision for the organization if elected. Open discussion with the full board should again follow until both the candidate and the board members feel clear for final action. The candidate and spouse are then dismissed from the meeting.

On behalf of the search committee, the search chair now offers the motion to elect the candidate as CEO. With either the by-laws or prior board action determining the majority required for election, a secret ballot is taken, and repeated if necessary until the decision is made. If the deciding vote is not unanimous, it is in order that a board member move that a vote of acclamation be cast to show the board's unity in its final decision.

When the action is completed, the candidate and spouse are invited back into the room for whatever response rises spontaneously from the board. At this moment, the board can seal the spiritual goal of the search by putting hands on the candidate or couple and joining together in a prayer of consecration. Like bookends, the prayer of consecration at the end of the process joins with the prayer of dedication at the beginning to seal the bond of relationship in the Body of Christ.

Note: In rare situations, the vote on the candidate is negative or the debate on the motion to elect the candidate is so fractious that to move forward to elect the candidate is unwise. In these instances, the search committee should be gracious and accept the failure to produce a qualified candidate. At this point, the search must be re-initiated either with the aid of the current search committee and consultant, if one was used, or a newly elected search committee and a new consultant.

Public Announcement

With the election of its CEO, the public relations goal for the search process comes fully into view as the search committee hands off this responsibility to the transition task force. As soon as the search committee is ready to present its recommended candidate to the board, the search chair will ask the communications or public relations member on the task force to proceed with planning for news releases and press conferences, both internal and external. In today's fast-moving electronic age, coordination of this release communication is vital.

Before any public announcement is made about the election of a CEO, the staff deserves first notice and first opportunity for celebration. The Christ-centered organization is an entity of its own, representing the Body of Christ with all of the emotions and reactions of the human family. So when a new CEO is elected by the board, let the celebration begin! God's people, in such a high hour, should be singing His praise, applauding His choice, and anticipating His future.

A Time to Celebrate

Nothing is more gratifying than to see the refining process of CEO search achieve its original goals. The *spiritual* goal has been realized in the unified sense of the will of God; the *leadership* goal has come to fruition in electing a leader whose gifts match the emerging needs of the organization; the *governance* goal has been shown in the collegial nature of the process; the *planning* goal has been achieved in the match between strategic priorities and leadership gifts and the *public relations* goal has been fulfilled by communicating the mission of the ministry through the election of its new chief executive leader. To God be the glory!

With All Due Diligence
Board Check
Electing God's Choice

As the search process comes to a conclusion and the board fulfills its sole authority for the election of the CEO, is the session guided by these steps:

	Yes	No
1. The board convenes in a regular or special session that coincides with a timely conclusion for the search process.	_____	_____
2. The board meets for election of the CEO in executive session.	_____	_____
3. Election of the CEO is the primary, if not the single, item on the agenda.	_____	_____
4. The search chair		
a. reviews the process,	_____	_____
b. cites the criteria from the Leadership Profile,	_____	_____
c. responds to board questions,	_____	_____
d. introduces the candidate and spouse (if applicable).	_____	_____
5. Board members have full and unhurried opportunity to ask and answer questions in interaction with the candidate.	_____	_____

6. After meeting with the candidate, the board:

   a. hears the report of the board chair on negotiations with the candidate, _____ _____

   b. receives the recommendation of the search chair as a motion to elect, _____ _____

   c. votes by secret ballot according to required majority, _____ _____

   d. if necessary, confirms the majority vote by acclamation, _____ _____

   e. welcomes back the CEO-elect, _____ _____

   f. consecrates the CEO-elect and spouse with a prayer of dedication, _____ _____

   g. notifies internal members of the ministry first, and _____ _____

   h. participates in a professionally-conducted press conference as the public announcement. _____ _____

Managing CEO Transition

Chapter 11

Managing CEO Transition
A Transforming Drama

CEO leadership transition means more than saying goodbye to a lame duck and anticipating the arrival of a fleet-footed gazelle. We cannot assume that the momentum of the organization will continue to fly on automatic pilot with the staff charging full speed ahead and the constituency applauding change without reservation. Nor can we assume that the board can sit back, shift into neutral, and await the recommendation of the search committee. A change of CEOs is a time of testing for the leadership of the board. The board has the responsibility to lead transition, manage change, maintain momentum, assure continuity for the mission, and prepare the way for the new leader.

The weight of this responsibility takes us back to the fact that CEO transition is an integral part of our sacred trust. Just as the search process begins with the spiritual goal of seeking the will of God in order to assure the witness of the Christ-centered community, so leadership transition is a spiritual charge for which we must have the discerning mind of the Spirit.

Managing Transition

The board is both manager and leader of this transition. Peter Drucker's oft-quoted words apply here: "Managers do things right; leaders do the right things." In the time of transition, a board has the dual obligation: doing things right and doing the right things.

As the first step in assuming its management responsibility, the board should consider appointing a transition task force to work with the search committee. Their duties run on parallel tracks. Whereas the search committee has the specific charge to recommend a candidate to the board, the transition task force has the broader charge to manage change, from the announcement of the outgoing CEO to the inauguration of the new leader. Most likely, this will involve several months of strenuous work. The task force needs a representative body of board members, administrators, staff and constituents. Its work will touch every phase of organizational and relational life, internal and external. The chair of the transition task force should be a board member. He or she is joined by two or three other colleagues from the board to show serious commitment to transitional matters and build *esprit de corp* among all with a vested interest in the future of the organization.

To send the signal that board leadership of CEO change is targeted and temporary, the transition task force would be organized with the following charge:

> *The Board authorizes the appointment of a representative transition task force with responsibility to assist the outgoing and incoming CEOs in personal transition, prepare the organization and its people for change, and plan events specifically related to leadership transition.*

To fulfill this charge, the Transition Task Force will perform these duties:

(a) assure a gracious conclusion to the tenure of the outgoing leader, including farewell events;

(b) assist the incoming leader on personal (spouse and family, if applicable) and professional matters related to the move, including welcoming events;

(c) recommend physical changes in the executive office and, if applicable, providing for the leader's family residence;

(d) plan for orientation/introductory sessions with organizational or constituent groups as requested by the incoming leader;

(e) develop a public relations plan for each stage of transition;

(f) serve as liaison between the board and the interim CEO to lay the groundwork and create the tone of organizational and relational readiness for change; and

(g) prepare a transitional budget to achieve the goals of leadership transition.

By doing these things properly in transition, the board will send the signal that the Christ-centered organization cares about people and knows how to celebrate its leadership.

The Interim CEO

CEO transition is the time when leadership development pays off. In-house candidates will be ready for an interim appointment under a CEO who is a model and mentor for emerging leaders. If an outgoing CEO has already named a person to serve as "second in command" or "executive in my absence," it is natural to ask that individual to continue in the role during transition. During a transition period, executive decisions will have to be made, CEO leadership will need to be visible, and legal matters may arise requiring executive title as well as authority. Bestowing the title of "Interim CEO" (or "Acting CEO") is appropriate as a show of confidence and a transfer of authority.

For prolonged periods of transition, such as a year or more, the individual may be appointed to a limited term as CEO. In these cases, the board and acting CEO must have a clear understanding of the time span for the role and the expectations for executive leadership during this time.

The role of the interim CEO can be summed up thus: to maintain the momentum and sustain the morale of the organization and its people. To introduce radical change during this time or to cast a long-term vision that the next leader will inherit is not within the parameters of either the interim CEO or the short-term CEO. This job means working hand in hand with the board to advance the mission through executive implementation of policy in partnership with the transition task force. The goal? To keep the constituency looking forward with hope.

Ideally, interim CEOs in Christ-centered organizations should generally see themselves in the company of John the Baptist, "preparing the way for the one who is to come."

Leading Transition

William Bridges, in his book *Transitions: Making Sense of Life's Changes,*[1] portrays the time of change as a three-act drama: (1) Old Endings; (2) Neutral Zone; and (3) New Beginnings.

Borrowing from Bridges' insight helps us anticipate the leadership role of the board during transition, especially as it relates to understanding the dynamics of organizational change. Envision CEO transition as a transformational drama in three acts: Act I – Taking Charge; Act II – Holding Steady; and Act III – Making Ready. In this drama, the Holy Spirit is the director, the board is producer, the organizational structure is the stage, the outgoing and incoming CEOs are the stars, members of the staff in the supporting cast, and the external constituency is the audience responding to the script with words and emotions.

---

[1] Decap Lifelong Books, Cambridge, Mass., 2004, 101-105.

Act I—Taking Charge

To open the transformational drama, the board steps forward to assume primary responsibility for leadership transition. This does not mean taking over the chief executive role that is still in the hands of the CEO who is leaving or has been transferred to the interim CEO. Rather, it means that the board takes charge of the strategy for what Bridges calls "Old Endings" in the transition. The first line of responsibility is to assist the constituency in "Letting Go" (Scene 1) of the past in an orderly and gracious process. Once that is underway, the board turns it attention to "Firming Up" (Scene 2). Open communication matched by clean decision-making are keys that reassure the staff that the board is in control and working for their best interest.

Act II—Holding Steady

According to Bridges, there is a period of time between "Old Endings" and "New Beginnings" described as "The Neutral Zone." Everything goes on hold until the signals of a new beginning are received. The use of "neutral" may describe some organizational settings, but in the Christ-centered organization where people are so committed to the ministry and to each other, the word is far too bland. Members of the organization do not coast through this zone; they experience and express strong emotions while waiting for the signs of forward movement. Again, it is the responsibility of the board to be the steadying force by "Relieving Anxiety" (Scene 1) in the constituency and "Reducing Ambiguity " (Scene 2) in the organization.

Act III—Making Ready

As the CEO selection process comes to a conclusion, the board exercises its leadership by making sure that all systems are Go for the new leader. Old baggage should not be transferred to the incoming CEO and delayed decisions should not be the starting point for the new administration. The board has the responsibility for "Operational Readiness" (Scene I) cultivated during transition so that the new CEO will have a solid base from which to meet the expectations for moving forward. Likewise, the board takes the lead for assuring "Relational Readiness" (Scene II) by bringing the constituents together in anticipation of new leadership. As transition comes to a close, the board joins the constituents in welcoming its new executive leader. An official ceremony of induction or inauguration is an act of celebration at which the Christ-centered organization excels. It is also the signal from the board that the transition is complete. At that moment, the board steps back from transitional leadership and invests its new CEO with the full authority and complete confidence required for success in the role.

With All Due Diligence
Board Check
A Transforming Story

Acknowledging responsibility for executive transition, the board exercises its authority by

	Yes	No
1. assuming the role as manager and leader of transition,	_____	_____
2. appointing a transition task force:	_____	_____
a. with a board chair and board members	_____	_____
b. representative of internal stakeholders	_____	_____
3. issuing a charge to the task force that is targeted, temporary and transitional,	_____	_____
4. foreseeing the potential of transition as a transformational drama,	_____	_____
5. anticipating the acts of transition:		
a. taking charge	_____	_____
b. holding steady	_____	_____
c. making ready	_____	_____
6. leading transition without blurring the lines between policy and execution, and	_____	_____
7. planning a clear exit strategy for the end of transition.	_____	_____

Chapter 12

Managing CEO Transition Taking Charge

Act I

In times of leadership transition, the board of a Christ-centered organization has to assume leadership responsibilities that would ordinarily be delegated to the CEO. This does not mean micro-managing or taking authority away from the incumbent or interim leader, but rather assuming responsibility for navigating the organization and its people through the shoals of change.

Letting Go

Scene 1

The work begins with the board giving personalized attention to the special dynamics of "letting go" in the Christ-centered organization and among Christian people. Responses to a change in leadership range from gladness to grief and from hostility to indifference. Anyone who has witnessed CEO transition will identify with one of the following profiles.

The Patriarch. Patriarchs who found Christ-centered organizations add a delicate dimension to CEO transition. The same entrepreneurial passion that accounts for a founder's success can also become a major obstacle to the organization's growth and vitality. Visionary leaders who start new nonprofits in response to an unmet need often bring a sense of "manifest destiny" to their founding role. They may run the danger of assuming that they alone can interpret the meaning of the organization in concert with the mind of God. That assumption brings the greater danger that their mission will be synonymous with their personal identity. Once the time comes to step aside, they have nothing left to live for. Sad story after sad story is told about esteemed founders of Christ-centered organizations who left their leadership position disillusioned in mind, broken in spirit, and vulnerable to sickness and even death.

Boards of Christ-centered organizations have a special responsibility to nurture their founders. Insight into the nature of organizational development is the starting point. Most organizations begin like a mom-and-pop grocery. Success depends on the passionate love and personal attention of the founder. Sooner or later, though, continuing growth in the business produces a supermarket that demands a governing board, an administrative structure, specialized skills and delegated responsibilities.

It is understandable that a founder is baffled by the change, feels lost in the system, and becomes convinced that his or her legacy is lost. One of the saddest sights is a founder wandering around offices of the ministry looking for affirmation, sitting in a side office pretending to be busy, demanding loyalty from old cohorts, or second-guessing the decisions of the new CEO. The board can help prevent this from happening. As an organization grows under its founder in size, staff, services, and budget, the board development programs should include sessions on the dynamics of organizational growth. Such sessions are best guided by a consultant. Without threatening the founder, an outside consultant can simply speak to the role of executive leadership in a changing system. At another timely moment in a board development series, a consultant can bring up the question of executive succession on the basis of principle rather than personality.

When the founder retires or is retired, every effort should be made to esteem the person, preserve the legacy, and assure continuity. It is wrong to do a "lateral sidestep" and put the founder into a meaningless role to soften the blow of retirement. This does not preclude that there may be a role for the founder that utilizes special gifts, but always under the authority of the new CEO. In one case, the board of an international mission organization gave the founder a free hand at the point of major gift contacts where his passion for the ministry was irreplaceable. Officially adopting the title of "Founder," the board gave him a distinctive honor that he accepted with new enthusiasm. Regretfully, however, he never learned to let go of the top position. Every time he touched down in the home offices, he reverted to his old role and cast his shadow over the light of his successor. Yes, there are cases where a clean, surgical cut is the only alternative to continuing hurt and bitterness.

The Prodigy. Christ-centered organizations are often beneficiaries of prodigious young leaders who would rise to the top in any field, secular or religious. After just a short time in office, they show the gifts of casting a vision, planning a strategy and seeing it implemented. The board often relaxes under the assumption that their leader has accepted a lifetime appointment. After all, who would want to leave a ministry while riding on the high tide? But the young leader who is a Prodigy will catch the attention of other Christ-centered organizations and invariably appear at the top of the list of prospects in CEO search. The more successful the CEO is, the more offers he or she receives. If the CEO moves on, however, he or she can leave behind a constituency that feels abandoned, loses a measure of self-esteem and expresses an edge of resentment. Accusations may fly that the individual used the organization as a stepping-stone. "Why," the people ask, "Aren't we good enough?" The constituents rarely takes pride in the advancement of its CEO to another organization. More often the board will have to address the emotions of resentment and the tendency to blame the board for the loss. It is up to the board to assure the constituents that the quality of CEO leadership will be continued.

Every search committee is looking for a Prodigy. They are few and far between. More than once, we have seen search committee members swept away by the charisma of an untested Prodigy. Dire consequences have followed for both the organization and the candidate. Yet there is not a tried and true way to predict the potential of a candidate for executive leadership before assuming office. The U.S. Army did extensive research into the predictors for future officers. All failed except for one non-scientific answer. When the candidates were put in a group setting, the one to whom the most people gravitated was also the one who had the best chance of success in future leadership! If there is any challenge for the future of leadership research, it is to identify those factors in prodigious young prospects that predict the potential for strong and effective Christian leadership.

The Achiever. Not all leaders of Christ-centered organizations have the aura of a Patriarch or the star power of a Prodigy, but there is no question about their effectiveness. These people are Achievers who plan carefully, set realistic goals, and get the job done. James McGregor Burns, in his book *Leadership,* identifies this kind of effectiveness as "transactional" rather than "transformational."[1] Working from the inside out and from the bottom up, transactional leaders accomplish just as much, sometimes more, than their transformational counterparts who lead from the outside in and from the top down.

Fifty years of observing CEOs, pastors, executive directors and other chief executives of Christ-centered organizations leads me to say that Achievers far outnumber Patriarchs and Prodigies. In fact, they may be the persons Jim Collins had in mind when he wrote about organizations where good things were happening without anyone taking the credit.[2] In these situations, Collins felt that we may see a glimpse of greatness. Like the fable Collins tells about the ever-scheming fox and the single-minded hedgehog, the hedgehog always wins.[3]

---

[1] *Leadership* (New York: Harper and Row, 1978), 4
[2] *Good to Great* (New York: Harper Collins Publishing, 2001), 27
[3] Ibid., 90-91

A retired military chaplain took over an ailing church. His background had taught him how to deal with a variety of situations in which the leader had to enter gently, proceed cautiously and exit on time. His pulpit was not particularly dynamic and he didn't try to overwhelm the board with a model of growing churches brought home from a seminar. Instead, he created a balanced and integrated ministry throughout the church and with his people. No magic button was pushed, but slowly the church began to grow with old and new generations coming together in hope. Soon, the word got out, the church was filled, and plans for enlargement were presented. This happened not once, but twice before the pastor retired again, not as a Patriarch or a Prodigy, but as an Achiever. Someplace in the halls of celebrated pastoral leaders, he has a niche.

The Caretaker. Christ-centered organizations are like human organisms that need to pause once in a while, particularly after the tenure of a Prodigy who runs fast and keeps heads spinning. The next CEO is often a person who brings a refreshing pause to the organization so that everyone can take a breath. Admittedly, the individual may be more manager (doing things right) than a leader (doing the right things). Sooner or later, however, the natives get restless and recall the exciting days when visionary leadership had everyone on the stretch. Because the Caretaker CEO is usually a likeable person, there will be rumblings below rather than rebellions above. So when the Caretaker leaves, there is just a communal shrug of indifference followed by a spark of anticipation for better days ahead. To reassure the constituents, the board must put high priority on the selection of a CEO who has the vision and drive to re-energize the organization.

The Bungler. Dismay clouds the climate of the Christ-centered organization that has to endure a leader whose gifts are mismatched with the needs and goals of the ministry. Nothing but compassion can follow CEOs who are thrust into leadership with demands beyond their gifts. More often than not, the Bungler is one who tries to do much too fast. Rather than heeding the sound advice to listen for six months before starting a revolution, the Bungler stamps in a vision before understanding the dynamics of the culture with both its limitations and its potential. Coming into office on the platform of change, the Bungler tromps on tradition, alienates people, and wastes resources.

Search committees can get at this problem by asking candidates, "What is your plan for the first six months in office?" One Bungler immediately proposed to move the headquarters for the ministry from the center of the city to the suburbs where he wanted to live. Another fired all of the executive staff. And another actually thought that acceptance in leadership would be accomplished by erecting a statue outside the entrance to his predecessor. Bunglers will have the traditional honeymoon in office and possibly coast on organizational momentum, but sooner or later, their lack of competence catches up and they fail on vision, mission, or strategy. When the Bungler leaves, there is a sigh of relief from a tolerant constituency, but not without the residual effect of disappointment. Often, Bunglers come from favorite sons or daughters of whom too much is expected. They excel as experts in their field or as friends in communal relationships, but fail when they are advanced to executive leadership where there are so many unknowns until the person is in the position. Christ-centered organizations are not exempt from Bunglers even when we claim divine appointment for the position. Most failures seem to be from mismatched or incompetent Bunglers. In such cases, the board must assure the constituency that careful attention will be given to selecting a CEO whose personal gifts match current and projected organizational needs. The board must also commit to nurture the growth of the next CEO, because no one comes to the office either skilled in all aspects of executive leadership or mature in all dimensions of personal development.

The Pariah. Leaders who are dismissed or resign on grounds of violating the trust of office send shock waves through the family of a Christ-centered organization. Although the number of cases is limited, the tragedy's magnitude challenges the leadership of the board. CEOs are especially vulnerable to the temptations that come with position and power. Derailment is not a lack of vision, a distortion of mission or a failure of strategy. Rather, Pariahs shoot themselves in the foot by moral, economic or relational failure. Each of us can cite an example of these failures—the CEO who goes through divorce in order to marry a staff member, the leader who indulges in lavish living at ministry expense, and the CEO who covers his tracks by lying to the board. Whatever the case, constituents go through a range of emotions: anger at the one whom they trusted, followed by remorse for a fallen member, ending with the desperate need to restore integrity in their midst. The challenge is out to the board to re-establish the principle of integrity in the mission even though an individual has failed. Coupled with that, the board must let the constituency know that compassion overrules vengeance in such tragic moments. If there is any recourse for restoring an individual or saving a family after dismissal or resignation, the board of a Christ-centered organization will choose that option.

We love Patriarchs, admire Prodigies, respect Achievers, tolerate Caretakers, pity Bunglers, and shun Pariahs. For good reason, then, we understand why the board of a Christ-centered organization has to nuance its response to the departure of its CEO. Whether a Patriarch, Prodigy, Achiever, Caretaker, Bungler or Pariah, the board walks the delicate line of integrity between the organization and the individual. Of course, if push comes to shove, the board's first responsibility is the integrity of the organization, but the individual cannot be forgotten. The story of every CEO becomes part of a "community of memory" for the organization. If the story is good, it should be honored for reinforcing the meaning of the mission; if it is bad, it should be used as a learning experience for future decisions. An effective board balances between being an engineer and an artist. The engineer's eye is on the details that must be addressed. At the same time, the artist's eye is on the big picture that can never be forgotten.

Firming Up

Scene 2

Change in CEO leadership is never the same twice. An astute board will review all of the factors going into transition and customize its leadership response. Yet there are some working principles for the board to consider in order to assure a clear and clean transition.

First and foremost, CEO transition is a time for the board to follow the three-fold rule: *Communicate, Communicate, Communicate.* A message of assurance from the board chair once or twice a month is the best way to let the constituency know that the board is in charge and cares about its people. With its ear to the ground, the board will also know when a special message is needed to alleviate doubts, fears, and false information.

Next, the board must be *open and honest in acknowledging the nature of transition.* Whether it is the retirement of a Patriarch, resignation of a Prodigy, departure of an Achiever, expiration of a Caretaker's term, termination of a Bungler or dismissal of a Pariah, the board must tell it like it is. It must do so without violating confidence, injuring the individual, or inviting litigation. Open and factual communication must be established early and continued throughout the transition. Fudging on the facts or talking down to the communicants is a sure way to lose the confidence of the constituency. Board members must always keep in mind the common commitment and mutual sacrifice that they share with administrators and staff of the Christ-centered organization.

In some instances, the board must be prepared for grief work. Every CEO transition is like a case of death and dying. Underneath the initial response from the constituency there may be feelings that follow the grieving process of denial, anger, and bargaining before acceptance that the leader is gone. These feelings are often directed against the board. When they are, the board must exercise understanding, patience, and counsel as the process unfolds. Again, open and honest communication is the best therapy for grief that comes from the loss of a leader, especially one who is beloved.

CEO transition is a special opportunity for a board to show the *meaning of grace*. It is easy to be gracious when a Patriarch or an Achiever is retiring, and by swallowing some pride, a board can bid farewell to a Prodigy. It is far more difficult to say good-bye to a Caretaker and almost impossible to find something good to say about a Bungler. It must be remembered, though, that each of these persons is now part of the history of the ministry, and unless their administration was a complete disaster, the board must do its best to salvage a career. In case after case, a failure in one ministry was followed by success in another. A pastor in a small parish had been dismissed by the bishop for incompetence. He changed denominations, moved north, and took a circuit of three small rural churches. A couple of years later, his superintendent said, "If you have any more people like Harold, send him along. He is the best." This is the lesson of a Spirit-guided match.

The dismissal of a Pariah puts grace to a special test. While the violation of trust can never be glossed over, the Christ-centered organization must be a place where repentance, forgiveness and restoration are always encouraged. While the integrity of the mission is the primary responsibility of the board, grace for a failed CEO must still be offered. Especially where a spouse and family are involved, if there is any option for protecting them and restoring the relationship with them, the board should be the first to encourage that action.

Finally, and most important of all, the board must *make a clean break in letting go of the CEO who retires, resigns or is dismissed.* For some reason, boards tend to go soft when it comes to making a clean cut with past CEOs. Stories abound about Patriarchs who retire with a golden parachute of benefits. Not too many years ago, CEOs truly served "at the pleasure of the board" with a handshake and a letter of appointment constituting the sum total of formal agreement. Today, with the terms of office negotiated prior to election and spelled out in detailed contracts, Achievers can be given severance pay and benefits that overlap their next appointment, Caretakers and Bunglers can add a lateral appointment within the organization or if retiring, be given an respectful title. Even Pariahs may have some recourse for remuneration through contractual agreement.

Boards often confer upon long term and effective CEOs such titles as chancellor, chairman, minister-at-large or CEO emeritus at the time of their retirement with a portfolio for public relations and fundraising. Office, staff, salary and benefits go with the appointment that may not have a limited term. It is not unusual for a board to decide prior to electing the new CEO and later, work out the details of the new relationship to the successor. In my own experience, I was courted for a university presidency where the outgoing Patriarch was retained as chancellor because of downtown and denominational connections. My first question was, "To whom will he report?" The secretary of the board answered, "We haven't decided yet." I told her to let me know when the decision was made before we talked again. She never called. Later I got word that a new CEO had been elected. Within two years, he resigned because he could never escape the shadow of the all-powerful chancellor.

At the very least, the board should defer on any title that includes a portfolio until the appointment of the new leader. If a relationship is agreed upon, it should still specify that the former leader report directly to the new CEO, require a specific job description for the role, limit the term of office, and not be included in board sessions except by invitation of the incumbent CEO. Even then, the relationship between new and old leaders is edgy. Over a period of time, a CEO who needs to establish his or her own identity may feel the lingering shadow of the past and want to change the relationship. Hurt feelings usually result.

In all of these cases, the board can save itself headaches by making a clean cut in its relationship with the outgoing CEO. If there is a rule of thumb that applies, the board needs to ask itself if its action encumbers the new CEO in any way that makes it harder to succeed or sends the signal that the organization is not yet ready for a new beginning. Letting go is the first task when a board takes charge of CEO transition. The way the board handles this task sets the tone and sends the message that a clear, clean, and positive change is ahead.

With All Due Diligence
Board Check
Taking Charge

With the announcement of CEO change, the board takes charge of transition by

	Yes	No
1. responding promptly with open and honest communication about the change,	_____	_____
2. customizing the process of "letting go" to the circumstances of the outgoing leader,	_____	_____
3. communicating regularly, internally and externally, with relevant information,	_____	_____
4. responding gracefully under all circumstances,	_____	_____
5. emphasizing the priority of mission over personality,	_____	_____
6. making a clean and clear break with the outgoing CEO,	_____	_____
7. avoiding any action handicapping the future leader,	_____	_____
8. creating an affirmative climate for change by looking forward.	_____	_____

Chapter 13

Managing CEO Transition
Holding Steady

Act II

After the initial impact of CEO change wears off, a wait-and-see period follows. A board may assume that this is a passing moment that will soon go away with the election of a new CEO, but it is an unrealistic expectation. The board must still lead during the in-between time when anxiety rises and ambiguity can rule.

Relieving Anxiety

During leadership transition, anxiety can spread through an organization like an infectious disease. When this happens, the health of the organizational body succumbs to such symptoms as fatigue, malaise, conflict and fear. Waves of anxiety ripple through an organization due to rumors or from the lack of communication from the board. Christ-centered organizations are particularly susceptible to anxiety due to close-knit relationships built around a common faith and bonded in the spirit of family. Moreover, unlike the employees in a secular corporation who only give a part of themselves to the enterprise, members of a Christ-centered organization make a total investment of mind, heart, and soul in its ministry. A vice president I recruited from a secular university taught me the difference. He came into my office and put his letter of resignation on my desk, saying that in the secular university members of the president's cabinet yelled and screamed at each other over administration issues. Afterwards, however, they would get together for a cup of coffee.

"In contrast," the vice president continued, "in the Christian organization, every issue we discuss and every decision we make is taken personally. I can't work this way." He put his finger on our strength as well as our weakness. We are a family living with the old reality, "You always hurt the ones you love." Among an organization's leaders—the formal or informal—a lack of trust or sense of doubt is contagious. In every CEO search where I have been a consultant, there has been a point when the search committee hears that there are doubts about their competence and sometimes their integrity. The charge should not be taken as a threat prompting a defensive reaction. Rather, it is a call for help from anxious people.

Anxiety rises in an organization when its people are not sure about the role that they will play in the future administration. Members of the executive team are particularly affected. Will we have a job? Will our administrative area be raised or lowered in value by the leader? Department heads will also feel the pressure. How will we fit in the new administration? Will our programs be considered essential or expendable? Anxiety runs deep, especially among those who feel distance between themselves and top administration. We have only veiled hints about the new CEO's priorities. How we will fit into the chain of command? What voice do we have in the process that may decide our destiny? Anxiety dominates the drama in Act II of CEO transition.

Consistency is the antidote to anxiety. When the board speaks and acts with consistency, the message of predictability relieves anxiety and renews the trust that is the glue for the Christ-centered constituency, whether in a local church, an educational institution, or parachurch ministry. During a CEO transition, the board's first responsibility in an anxious climate is to *speak with a calming voice.*

Boards themselves can succumb to panic in anxious times. Mixed signals are bad, but anxious acts are worse. In one case when a prodigious young leader moved on, the board offered significant bonuses to executive team members who were willing to stay on. The board learned that you cannot buy commitment. Those who wanted to leave left and those who wanted to stay stayed. Moreover, the payment sent an anxious signal through the organization and raised a question among other administrators and staff who were equally committed but not compensated.

Most important of all, the board needs to *restate its promise of predictability in a time of transition.* A leader who wants to build trust will say to his or her followers, "I will do exactly as I say I will, and if I change my mind, you will be the first to know." The same principle applies to board leadership when dealing with anxiety during CEO change. Of course, the principle will be tested because the board is not omniscient on every issue. Still, if the principle is stated, restated, and consistently enacted, the message will get through. After that, the board will have to count on a common commitment to a common mission to prevail.

Reducing Ambiguity

Organizational ambiguity is the companion of personal anxiety in a time of transition. Even in the organization that continues to function effectively, there is the lurking sense that policies, priorities, programs and procedures may be up in the air. Who knows how things may change? How will power be redistributed? How long do we have to wait to see? How can I be creative in the midst of uncertainty? The lack of surety creates a vacuum into which seven demons rush. Worse yet, saboteurs can take advantage of the vacuum to undermine the organization's purpose and spirit. How does the board respond to this threat?

Just as anxiety is relieved by consistency, ambiguity is reduced by clarity. First and foremost, the board must *reaffirm the identity or position of the organization.* CEO transition has a way of opening the cracks in our organizational self-identity. If we are not sure who we are and why we exist, leadership transition will expose these weaknesses. The person who suggested that every board meeting begin with the motion to dissolve the organization was not playing games. The board of a Christ-centered ministry must be able to give a current answer to the questions, "Why do we exist?" and "If we did not exist, would we have to be invented?" This is the time for the board to ask these questions aloud, of its own members. Then it goes public to give the 60-second elevator speech that has continuity across generations of boards and executives. Failing to give that speech, the board defaults on its leadership. It adds to the uncertainty of the moment.

"Why do we exist?" is a valid question that board members need to ask and answer. In board development sessions, board members may be asked to give that 60-second elevator speech answer to each other while being timed on a stop-watch. The results are mixed on the first run, but then when the roles of speaker and listener are reversed, statements begin to take focus. It especially needs to be answered during leadership transition when identity, integrity, and indispensability need to be reaffirmed.

In support of the organization's identity, the board needs to *restate the primary policies that lead the organization.* For example, historical, theological and philosophical deviations will not be tolerated, and missional compromises will not be accepted. Saboteurs who think that CEO transition is the time to undermine the position or policies of the organization will get the message.

Throughout the transition period beginning with the announcement of leadership change through the inauguration of the new CEO, there will be gaps in understanding that add to the problem of ambiguity. An alert board can get ahead of these challenges by *clarifying its position on each step as the transition goes forward.* As noted earlier, the search process requires confidentiality as well as flexibility. Clarity is again the key. For example, during the search process, the board will have to remind all its stakeholders that the board alone is responsible for the election of the CEO. Or, after the election but before the new CEO takes office, the board must make it clear who is still in authority. Clarity in these matters is one of the keenest tools in the leadership kit of a board.

Leadership transition produces a vacuum of power that begs to be filled. Like the man from whom Jesus cast a demon, unless the void is filled by positive forces, there are seven demons waiting to enter. The board, by affirming its leadership in the transition process, will fill the void and leave no room for demons that thrive on ambiguity.

Building Anticipation

Leadership of the board in the time of transition means managing hope. Anxiety and ambiguity are best dispelled by looking forward. The board can do this by *showing that the organization is on track with its vision.* Showing achievement in its strategic goals makes a strong case for continuity. Focus is kept on the big picture with the board leading the way leaning forward into the future. More specifically, the board foresees new opportunities to be grasped, rewards creative people, commends staff for adapting to transition, and confesses how it is learning as it leads. Even small wins count. Achievement of a balanced budget, a major gift, an enterprising program, testimonies of grateful people, public or professional recognition for the organization or one of its members—these are all meaningful symbols of momentum.

Speaking of symbols, the board also must *lead proactively in setting the tone.* Anxiety and ambiguity are forces that take on a life of their own, and they will unless boards take on the responsibility for being tone-setters. This does not mean sugar-coating communications or over-spiritualizing conflict. It does mean that every member of the board becomes a tone-setter in formal and informal communication. Realistic optimism is the message that staff hears from its board.

Reports are read, not just for content, but the spirit that they convey. Sentences are written with the question in mind, "What's between the lines?" Board chairs, in particular, lead with more than words when they seek to relieve anxiety or reduce ambiguity. Their facial and body language speaks volumes. Consistency that relieves anxiety and clarity that reduces ambiguity must be communicated from the inside out. When words are matched with emotions in a message of hope, leadership is at its best.

As the master of symbols big and small, the board can do more than just hold steady. By crafting its words, showing its face, and saying "Thank you," it can transform the anxiety and ambiguity of Act II into the anticipation that characterizes an organization that is learning and growing as it changes.

With All Due Diligence
Board Check
Holding Steady

During the in-between period of CEO transition, our board is holding steady by:

	Yes	No
1. being alert for signs of anxiety in the organization.	_____	_____
2. responding to the signs with sensitivity.	_____	_____
3. communicating with a calming voice.	_____	_____
4. giving assurance by personal presence.	_____	_____
5. providing anxious people with the opportunity to express themselves.	_____	_____
6. reinforcing its promise of predictability.	_____	_____
7. reaffirming the identity of the organization.	_____	_____
8. restating the guiding policies.	_____	_____
9. repeating the progressive steps of transition.	_____	_____
10. using symbols of hope to set the tone for change.	_____	_____

Chapter 14

Managing CEO Transition
Making Ready

Act III

As the final act of the transformational drama unfolds, one question absorbs the board. "What can we do to prepare the way for the new leader?" Answers come under the theme "readiness." If the board has been effective in taking charge of transition (Act I) and holding steady during anxious times (Act II), its final task will be to consolidate the gains that were learned during the process (Act III). The proof of those gains will show how ready the organization and its people are for new executive leadership.

Two additional questions set the stage for Act III. First, is the organization functionally ready for change? Second, are the people psychologically ready for new leadership? Answers to these questions will tell whether or not the board has been effective in leading the transition, engaging the staff, and meeting the challenge of change.

Operational Readiness

Scene 1

As the time of transition moves toward the end, our goal is to have all systems ready to fire on all cylinders. Too often, however, boards sit back and do nothing but hope that the new leader will ride in like a white knight to jump start the organization. As we have already noted, transition naturally creates a temporary lag in organizational momentum. Ideally there is little time between when one CEO leaves and the new CEO arrives. In situations where there is significant time between the departure and arrival dates, with or without an interim leader, the board chair will need to be alert to signs of loss of momentum.

Every new leader is in for some surprises. Between the lines of the Leadership Profile there will be facts and feelings that cannot be known until the new leader is in office. Financial surprises are frequent because of the complexity of budgets, accounting practices and financial statements. Even more frequent is discovering internal dynamics that do not come up in information sessions. Only when the chief executive makes decisions does he or she learn where the rocks are and where there are undercurrents beneath the surface. There is a difference between internal dynamics that test leadership skills and those that can bring an organization to a standstill.

Symptoms of a slowed or stalled organization are readily seen. *The tell-tale sign is a shift of focus and energy from serving people to saving the organization.* These secondary symptoms immediately follow:

- Attitudes shift from creativity to conservation

- Focus is upon process rather than substance

- Rewards are based on morale rather than performance

- Ideological positions trump facts

- Bureaucracy rules

Boards should not become too aggressive during transition. One organization went through a deep schism when the CEO was dismissed. So the board stepped in to take an active role in operations and had direct involvement with the staff in administrative decisions. Hoping to resolve the rift, a complete remake of governance was put in place. Consequently, the boundaries for executive search were narrowed to candidates who fit the revised style. By taking such aggressive action in the time of crisis, the board changed the character of the organization and its leadership.

Between the two extremes, the board must *lead in keeping the focus of the organization upon those whom it is called to serve.* Without being too passive or too aggressive, the board is like a master sailor who has a light hand on the tiller and keeps the ship moving on course. As a guide for this role, the board asks itself some key questions:

- Are we unified in our understanding of our mission?

- Are we seeing the same vision for the future?

- Are the lines clear between policy development and executive implementation?

- Are we agreed on our expectations for executive leadership?

- Are our lines of communication open throughout the organization?

- Are the administrators in each area functioning effectively?

- Are the standards for fiscal accountability being followed?

- Are the employees finding meaning in their work?

- Are those we serve satisfied?

- Are constituent stakeholders confident of the future?

- Does the organization have credibility in its profession and the larger public?

If a board must answer "No" to these questions or express doubts, it has not done its job of developing policy, overseeing executive leadership or managing ambiguity during transition. The board that answers "Yes" has laid the foundations to attract top-quality leadership and assure a running start into the future.

Relational Readiness

Scene 2

Everything is about relationships in the Christ-centered organization. Beginning with a personal commitment to Jesus Christ and bringing a sense of divine calling to their task, every member at every level finds common ground. Like Paul's image of the organic Body of Christ in II Corinthians, the Christ-centered organization has a sense of oneness and wholeness that is its richest resource. But all is not perfect. Because of the depth of interpersonal relationships, the staff can be most fragile, especially during leadership transition for top leadership. As we saw in Act II, the board must understand the unique nature of its organization and respond with sensitivity to its relational needs. Business members of the board who are successful in secular organizations may find it frustrating to work with such a heavy emphasis upon relationships, but they bring objectivity to balance issues heavily weighted toward emotion and anxiety.

All organizations have some of the characteristics of a family, and the Christ-centered organization is best understood using that model. As we remember from Tolstoy's opening line of Anna Karenina, "All happy families are alike; every unhappy family is unhealthy in its own way." We can immediately think of the many ways that organizational families are unhappy.

- Leadership is oppressive, disconnected and contradictory
- Cohesion gives way to schism
- Reactive members use anxiety to take the family hostage
- Conflict is a willful tactic
- Creative members are marginalized
- Direct communication is replaced by triangles
- Scapegoats are blamed for problems
- Outsiders are unwelcome

Board members need to be alert for the red flags of these symptoms. When the *attention of the staff shifts from internal cohesion to interpersonal conflict, the family is in deep trouble.* If cohesion, the greatest strength of the Christ-centered organization, is fractured, then staff morale is shattered. Oftentimes, the schism can be created by a small clique or one dysfunctional individual who takes the organization hostage by exploiting anxiety, sabotaging innovation, casting blame, alienating friends, and hiding behind "spiritual" motives. If Christ-centered organizations have a vulnerable spot, it is using spirituality as a defense mechanism for system failures, personal vendettas, confrontational cowardice, poor decisions, and just plain incompetence. In such cases, the strength of close relationships in the Christ-centered organization can become its weakness, especially during the time of CEO transition.

Board leadership can help prevent such fractures by communicating the message *"We are all in this together."* But such words must be backed up. The board must show itself as a cohesive unit and see itself as one in mission and spirit with the organization. Otherwise, the voice of unity has the sound of a hollow gong. Simply calling for a vote of acclamation on critical issues or pledging to keep confidence about board decisions are worthy but futile attempts to show unity. If a board is divided, it will be exposed. Read the eyes, listen to the inflection of the voice, and watch the expression on the face of a dissenting board member. Unified action must follow unified words.

Boards do have some resources for keeping Christ-centered organizations glued together. One is the *common spiritual commitment.* There is no substitute for the board joining in times of devotion, communion and consecration with all members of the organization. Another resource is a retreat-type setting in which the board becomes one among the members discussing the vision, mission and strategy for the organization. Still another resource is a *professional tool* such as The Best Christian Workplaces survey. It identifies where the organization is comparatively weak or strong on relational as well as operational measures. At times, *outside consultation*—or even an "insultant"—may be needed, but a board cannot forfeit its own leadership responsibility by engaging an expert. If there is relational fracture, the board must give full support to the executive leader, whether interim or permanent, to take the action necessary to deal directly with dysfunctional members or cliques. Opinions will differ on how the board takes action on these malcontents, especially during leadership transition. Timely but gracious confrontation cannot be avoided, and if there is no resolution, dismissal may be the only alternative.

Reprise

Operational readiness and relational readiness go hand in hand. Research by The Best Christian Workplaces Institute shows that organizations with a high correlation between Christian character and professional competence top the list for places where morale is high, workers are satisfied, operations are efficient, and needs are served. The true legacy of leadership is to give your successor accelerators that speed your organization on to even greater things. These accelerators include:

1. **Missional integrity**—theological, philosophical and historical congruence with the mission of the organization;

2. **Visionary flexibility**—strategic options for timelines and tactics based upon changing external and internal circumstances;

3. **Organizational momentum**—a sense of movement leaning forward into the future with energy and enthusiasm;

4. **Communal morale**—a transparent climate created by clear decisions and open communication in which people can grow and issues can be resolved;

5. **Financial discipline**—an annual budget process matched by a long-term plan to assure the economic viability of the organization;

6. **Transferable loyalty**—evidence that key persons serving and supporting the organization are primarily committed to the mission rather than a person.

Although the sum of these accelerators makes an ideal situation for new executive leadership, they also serve as dashboard indicators for the board to assess the operational and relational vitality of the organization at any time. Rather than waiting until the end of transition to score the organization on the these factors, they are more valuable as part of an ongoing assessment. The most effective board is always alert for the key indicators of a healthy organization. Squeezed down to the essentials, the board will continually ask, "Is the vision clear?" "Is the mission firm?" and "Is the tone positive?" Affirmative answers will bring the transformational drama to a close with the good word that the organization is operationally and relationally ready to welcome its new CEO.

Once the new CEO takes office, it might be assumed that the work of transition is over. In many instances, that is the case. The board withdraws, the transition task force dissolves and the new leader is left to fly solo.

We need to revise that viewpoint. If the new CEO wishes, the board should authorize and fund the continuation of the transition task force for the first six months to a year of the new administration. Rather than leaving the CEO alone to listen, plan, discriminate, understand, and act in the new organizational setting, the transition task force can be eye, ear, heart, and hand in providing a smooth entry for their leader. A CEO willing to work with an extended transition task force has an invaluable resource at hand. Having played an integral role in the transformational drama, the transition task force will have sensors deep in the organizational culture that a new CEO, working alone, would take months to develop and read. As an assist for the new leader, the continuing transitional task force could perform such functions as: (1) orienting the new CEO to the organizational culture, its mores, values, rituals, sensitivities, expectations and informal flow

123

of power; (2) introducing the new CEO to key persons and places within and without the organization; (3) listening for feedback to the CEO's initial statements of vision, reports on decisions, and meetings with groups; (4) providing a personal, confidential base for prayer support on transitional issues; (5) assuring the adjustment of the new CEO and family to their personal, family and office needs; (6) hosting relaxed social settings for the CEO and family with board members, ministry staff, church and community groups; and (7) helping the board and staff understand the new CEO as a person, a Christian, and a leader.

A continuing transition task force should have a clear exit strategy developed with the CEO. Sending the signal that the transition is over and a relationship of trust has been established with the leader, personally, professionally, and spiritually proves valuable. At that moment, the Christ-centered organization is ready to move ahead with the board and staff reading off the same page as their CEO.

With All Due Diligence
Board Check
Making Ready

As the board of a Christ-centered organization, how ready are you for the arrival of your new CEO?

	Readiness Rating				
	Not Ready		Somewhat Ready		Very Ready
1. Missional integrity	1	2	3	4	5
2. Visionary flexibility	1	2	3	4	5
3. Organizational momentum	1	2	3	4	5
4. Communal morale	1	2	3	4	5
5. Financial discipline	1	2	3	4	5
6. Transferable loyalty	1	2	3	4	5

What other readiness factors would you include on this scale that apply specifically to your Christ-centered organization? How do you rate yourself on these additional factors?

Chapter 15

Managing CEO Transition
A Transformational Moment

One final note is sounded when the Christ-centered organization goes through the transformational drama of leadership transition. It is the note of celebration when the new executive is officially inducted into office. Although he or she may have already assumed the position and begun work, a time must be set aside for an inauguration to capture this high moment. No other occasion so readily lends itself to internal bonding and external branding for the Christ-centered organization. The advent of new executive leadership is the time for celebration when an astute board exercises transitional leadership one last time.

Internal Bonding

Think about leadership transition as a special advantage for building and celebrating the internal cohesion of the Christ-centered organization. At one organization, an accrediting team commended the spirit of community in their report: "We have never seen a place that finds so many reasons to celebrate." The team was referring not just to official dinners but also to the monthly staff meetings to celebrate birthdays, brides and babies. To paraphrase a common saying, "The community that celebrates together, stays together."

The induction or inauguration of a new CEO builds upon the spirit of celebration in the Christ-centered organization. Whether limited to a day or extended over a period of time, the board must take the lead in this. An ad hoc induction or inauguration committee, separate from the transition task force and the selection committee should be appointed with a budget sufficient to bring the constituency together in celebration. It is the special moment for thanking God for the person He has chosen to lead the organization into the future.

Internal bonding is the primary goal of inaugural celebrations. Formal events such as an inauguration in a Christian university, an induction ceremony in a parachurch organization, or a service of consecration in a local church, all bring the constituency together in a celebratory mood. Each of these should be balanced by some kind of family gathering in which the new CEO is presented as human, vulnerable, and authentic. This is also the time for the staff to re-consecrate itself to the call of God and its vision for ministry. As always, the board must lead the way.

The board can also use this time to commit itself to the professional development of its people. Seminars or workshops on career development and professional competencies are powerful tools for letting employees know that they are valuable and esteemed.

Think, then, of the full potential for internal bonding when a new leader is inducted or inaugurated. People can get to know their chief executive as a person, not just an occupant of a high position; individuals at all levels of responsibility can have their ministry affirmed; and as the oneness of spirit is strengthened, self-esteem is lifted for both the individual and the organization.

External Bonding

Christ-centered organizations often invest significant dollars to present themselves to those they serve or want to serve. But the cost-benefit of these investments is seldom assessed. It is like the pill that you take without knowing the results but have to keep taking just in case. Media advertising is a game that everyone feels compelled to play. Yet a quick scan of the ads and websites show little difference in the branding of comparable ministries. The market merges into mush.

Think then about the introduction of a new chief executive into the public market. Even though it comes around only once in a while, it is the story that stands out for special attention. It can also be the most economical and effectual means for branding the organization in the minds of both religious and secular publics. In fact, done right, it can be almost free.

Public ceremony. A board that has worked through the three acts of the transformational drama has all of the ammunition needed to send out a formal announcement that begins, "On behalf of the board ... you are invited to be our guest for the induction of .... as our new CEO." A concise statement of the mission of the organization and brief biography of the new leader along with the schedule of events, guest tickets, directions, parking passes, and an RSVP card in first-class style are hard to ignore. Even if the recipient declines the invitation, the introduction has been made.

The purpose is to make the public ceremony a memorable event. It both highlights the new leader and showcases the ministry. A common format is a speaker of note along with a charge from the board followed by a visionary response from the new leader. These messages can be complemented by first-person testimonies or video presentations that illustrate the ministry in action. Once the guests have been introduced to the mission, leadership, and effectiveness of the organization, the imprint opens the door for further contacts and involvement.

Media presentations. The introduction of a new chief executive tests the media effectiveness of the public relations or communications staff as well. Contacts with key persons in both the secular and religious media should have been cultivated over time so that the network can be readily tapped for the introduction of the new leader and related events. Instead, we often find media relationships limited to a narrow band of evangelical connections. Most communication is like preaching to the choir. Stringers to news services and face-to-face, name-to-name media contacts should be part of the vision for advancing the ministry of the Christ-centered organization. Without cultivating these contacts and relationships, press conferences may be called and no one comes.

Furthermore, a little creativity uncovers numerous sources for free publicity when a new leader is announced. Certain Christian media outlets provide a regular listing announcing appointments in the evangelical community. Add to that the untapped potential for posting the appointment on websites, blogs, and networking sites. Every one of these media sources is a tool in our hands.

Strategic presence. A schedule of strategic touch points should be included as part of the plan to introduce a new CEO. National conferences, service clubs, civic events, professional societies, denominational meetings, and evangelical associations are natural settings for the introduction. It may be a speaking engagement, a display table, an invocation, or a personal introduction by a board member. All count in the celebration of new leadership. Contacts with constituents and primary stakeholders come first, but the plan should not be limited to them. The advent of a new leader opens the door for a Christ-centered organization to extend its witness in the public sphere.

"Strategic" is the word for all of these contacts. The new leader's time and energy cannot be wasted, but in the opening days, weeks and months of a new administration, there is a window of opportunity for external branding that swings wide open. Because it closes so quickly, we dare not miss the moment.

So, as the final curtain falls on the transformational drama of executive transition, the leader is on center stage, the cast surrounds its star, stage hands are in the wings, and the public is applauding. Someplace in the audience, however, it is the board that has the satisfaction of being the producer behind the scenes, never forgetting that the director of the drama is none other than the Holy Spirit.

With All Due Diligence
Board Check
A Transformational Moment

In celebration of God's good will, our board introduces our new leader by:

	Yes	No
1. authorizing a commissioning or inaugural committee with board leadership;	_____	_____
2. announcing a time of commissioning or inaugural celebration;	_____	_____
3. approving an adequate budget for inaugural events;	_____	_____
4. bonding with the organization's staff and constituency;	_____	_____
5. advancing professional self-esteem at all levels in the organization;	_____	_____
6. joining in events that show the human side of leadership;	_____	_____
7. supporting a public relations plan for external branding;	_____	_____
8. leading a public ceremony of commissioning or inauguration;	_____	_____
9. introducing the new leader through personal networks of board members; and	_____	_____
10. making the introduction the exit point for board leadership of transition.	_____	_____

Leading
CEO
Development

Chapter 16

Leading CEO Development
A Nurturing Network

Leadership is a gift that board members have a sacred trust to uphold. When the board of a Christ-centered organization exercises its authority to elect its CEO, its responsibility does not end. In fact, it just begins. Because leadership is bestowed by God, we must do more than select and elect our CEO. God expects us to both cultivate the potential and nurture the promise of our elected leader as he or she matures in Christian character and executive competence.

What seems obvious in theory is often contradicted in practice. Some secular corporations are notorious for recruiting the most talented leaders for their CEOs, exploiting their gifts, exhausting their energies, and dropping them to a soft landing with a golden parachute. In recent years, we have seen CEO compensation go through the roof with salaries, options, benefits, incentives, and perks. This is "throw-away leadership" at its worst. Christ-centered organizations have not been exempt from the influence. In a radical reversal from times past when we kept our CEOs poor to keep them pure, some Christ-centered organizations have adopted the corporate mentality for excessive executive compensation. Someplace along the line, the sense of call and commitment gets lost, especially when lower levels of staff are working at sacrifice, even on survival margins. Most Christ-centered organizations, however, are not guilty of this sin of commission. Our boards are more culpable for the sin of omission, namely, to elect a CEO and then say, "Now you are on your own."

Case after case can be cited in which the board functions as absentee landlords, dipping into board meetings, governing in the comfort zone of financial matters, and as long as things are going well, rubber stamping the recommendations of the CEO. If we really believe that leadership is a rare gift for which we have a sacred trust, doing this is wrong. When a person makes a life commitment under the call of God to become chief executive, the board owes that person a parallel commitment. This commitment is to nurture his or her personal and professional growth in a maturing model of leadership. With this view of leadership, we witness to the organizational world. We esteem our executive when we acknowledge leadership as a rare gift of God, accept responsibility for that gift, and make the commitment to see him or her rise to full potential.

The Creation Ethic

If leadership is a rare gift and in a Christ-centered organization the board has responsibility for that gift as a sacred trust, how do we steward our responsibility for its growth? The question takes us back to the creation story in which God gives Adam the guidelines for stewarding the physical and human resources that were in his trust. Physical, relational, intellectual and spiritual resources make up God's gifts of creation.[1]

Physical resources include matter, time, space and energy. They stand apart from other resources because they are subject to the Law of Entropy, meaning that they run down as they are used. To be stewards of these resources, God expects us to "cultivate and conserve" all physical resources, whether as stewards of our space, our money, our time or our energy. Because these resources are running down, we must use them wisely in order to realize their full potential.

God's gifts of relational, intellectual and spiritual resources differ from physical resources because they do not run down when they are

---

[1] *Good Stewardship*, David L. McKenna (Association of Governing Boards, 1991) Chapter 1

used. Rather they are subject to the Law of Syntropy, meaning that they grow and gain quality as they are exercised. Relational resources in the Creation story include human companionship, marriage, vocation, and family. God puts Adam's intellectual resources to work in the task of naming all of the animals. Because naming means control, we sense the power of intellect and the confidence of God in making Adam the master of all animals. Spiritual resources are at the highest level of all when God and man are in communication, enjoying each other's presence, and extending that relationship to others. A whole new world of opportunity and responsibility opens up for us. Holding fast to the principle of "conserve and cultivate," the mantra is "exercise and enjoy." Along with the willingness to make the effort comes a degree of freedom that makes our investment in the relational, intellectual, and spiritual growth of a leader so rewarding.

Two working principles from the creation ethic guide the board of a Christ-centered organization in nurturing its CEO. One, for the limited physical resources of personal well-being, money, time, energy and space susceptible to decline upon use, the principle is "conserve and cultivate." Two, for the relational, intellectual and spiritual gifts that are unlimited and open to qualitative increase upon use, the principle is "exercise and enjoy." When a plan for nurturing our executive's natural gifts includes these two principles, the goal of a maturing leader is well within our sights.

Growing a Leader

The term "board member" takes on new meaning when we accept our responsibility for nurturing executive leadership. It means that God trusts us to be stewards (or managers) of all of the gifts that He has given to our leader, not just his or her physical welfare in a compensation package. To be in trust also means that God holds us accountable for both conserving the physical gifts and investing in the relational, intellectual, and spiritual gifts of our leader. What a privilege! When the board adopts this biblically-based view of its responsibility and opportunity, it finds new meaning and satisfaction in its work. But, more than understanding and acceptance of our sacred trust is required. To fulfill that trust, we must nurture leadership as a priority task of intentional design.

Five connections in a nurturing network open before us. To honor our trust, we will see our work in these relationships:

- Raising the bar

- Compensating a commitment

- Partnering with potential

- Pushing the envelope

- Measuring wholeness

In these growth stages we see a process of development similar to the one outlined by the Apostle Paul in his second letter to Timothy, "All scripture is God-breathed and useful for teaching, rebuking, correcting and training is righteous" (II Timothy 2:16-17). The same passage gives us the goal for nurturing our executive leader, "... so that the man of God may be thoroughly equipped for every good work." With this perspective in mind, being a board member for a Christ-centered organization takes on new dimensions with renewed meaning. To see the organization's mission fulfilled at the same time that the CEO is becoming a maturing model of leadership is what makes board membership infinitely worthwhile.

With All Due Diligence
Board Check
A Nurturing Network

In keeping with our commitment to the CEO we have elected, our board:

	Yes	No
1. defines "trustee" and "stewardship" from a biblical base;	_____	_____
2. accepts nurturing the CEO as one of our priorities;	_____	_____
3. recognizes that our board's commitment to our CEO is just as important as our CEO's commitment to the board;	_____	_____
4. takes a "conserve and cultivate" approach to physical resources, including the well-being of the CEO;	_____	_____
5. assumes an "exercise and enjoy" attitude toward the relational, intellectual and spiritual resources for CEO leadership;	_____	_____
6. works with a comprehensive personal growth plan for our CEO that includes:		
a. setting benchmarks for growth;	_____	_____
b. assuring support for professional well-being;	_____	_____
c. building board-CEO relationships;	_____	_____
d. stretching relational, intellectual, and spiritual limits for personal development; and	_____	_____
e. assessing progress toward goals.	_____	_____

Chapter 17

Leading CEO Development
Raising the Bar

To honor our sacred trust for presidential nurture, it cannot be an incidental, casual or occasional task for a board. Leadership development, in any context, must be intentional and continual. The board that takes this charge seriously will write a firm commitment to its executive leader into its list of responsibilities and organizational structure.

An intentional commitment. Board duties are defined in the by-laws of the corporation. There is never any doubt that only the board has authority "To elect the CEO." To declare its intention to develop the gifts of its executive leader, the board needs to make it for real. It can either expand this statement or create a separate item that reads, "To nurture the CEO." Otherwise, the task will fall between the cracks. Some boards may be more specific, and state, "To elect, support, nurture, and evaluate the CEO." The advantage of that statement is that both the board and its executive leader know what to expect and are obligated to put a plan into action.

An organizational assignment. After putting its responsibility for CEO development in writing, the board needs to decide how to go about it. It may locate this task either within its existing structure or in a special committee. Quite naturally, the task falls under the duties of the executive committee of the board. This is a logical decision because the executive committee meets frequently and can assure the continuity of leadership development. The problem is that the agenda of the executive committee can be so full that nurturing the leader gets shunted into second place and loses its priority for action. Especially when things are going well, there is the tendency to leave well enough alone or adopt the attitude "If it ain't broke, don't fix it." In either case, the nurturing role is lost. Leadership development is the preventative for executive crisis, not the remedy.

A committee on executive development has the advantage of making sure leadership development stays at the top of the board agenda. The obvious disadvantage is one more committee that needs to be chaired, staffed, serviced and given time for deliberation and reporting.

Another option is to include CEO development in a committee on governance. This committee would also have responsibility for developing board members and the assessing board performance. Whatever structure the board chooses, the test is whether or not CEO leadership gets the time and attention it deserves.

A specific charge. Once the commitment to CEO development has been assigned, the board needs to formulate the specific details of the assignment. A sample charge might read: *To develop and implement a growth plan with our CEO that takes into account personal and professional needs, opportunities, and goals in support of maturing and effective Christian leadership.* This charge might also include the committee to whom the charge is made and a timeline for reporting back to the board. If desired, more detailed expectations can be part of the plan itself, as long as the expectations are developed mutually between the CEO and the board chair or representative committee.

A key relationship. Even though a specific committee is charged to develop a growth plan for the leader, the board chair and the CEO must work together to personalize the growth plan. Actually, this relationship begins back in the search when the board chair becomes acquainted with the future leader on a one-to-one basis. After election, the relationship advances another step when the terms of agreement are negotiated between the two. At that time, the board chair will hear the heartbeat of the CEO-elect on such matters as family, housing, health care, life insurance, and professional expenses. In turn, the CEO will be able to decipher how sensitive the board chair is to less tangible aspects of leadership development, such as vacation time, avocational interests, sabbaticals, church and community interests, and professional advancement goals. Out of these conversations, the board chair and CEO bond together naturally in a team relationship of mutual trust that is absolutely essential to executive nurture. If this trust is not established, it is doubtful that any plan for leadership development can succeed.

The board chair/CEO relationship is the key to nurturing executive leadership because of the continuity of contact. Most CEOs have a conversation with their board chairs at least once a month. With a finger on the pulse of the organization as well as its leader, the board chair is in the best position to encourage growth, implement the plan, and read the signs of gain or loss. Even if the board chair is not expected to "ride point" on CEO development, he or she will be instrumental to its success.

The starting point. CEO development is neither a hit or miss commitment for the board nor a do-it-yourself kit for their leader. A plan that matches the future needs of the organization with the growth potential of the individual works to the benefit of all parties. Goals for the plan must be realistic, time-sensitive and measurable.

The best place to start is the Leadership Profile. This was the finely-tuned plan that guided the search to make the selection of the CEO. Because no candidate is perfect, the search committee had to choose the person who was the best fit for the position from among other qualified candidates. Comparative strengths versus weaknesses among the prospects for the position had to be weighed and ranked in order to come to the decision. But, as one wise CEO said, "We are elected for our strengths, but judged by our weaknesses." If the board closes its eyes to the areas of weakness where its leader needs to grow, it will fail to follow through with its sacred trust.

A Case in Point

"It's a stunning opportunity." These italicized words drew immediate attention to the announcement of an opening in the presidency of a Christ-centered organization. A quick glance at the expectations for the CEO showed why the opportunity was so stunning. Primary roles for the new leader included:

> Vision casting
>
> Team leadership and program/operations oversight
>
> Board relations
>
> Strategic planning
>
> Champion of the vision, mission and core values
>
> Fundraising and resource development
>
> Public relations and advocacy

As idealistic as these expectations may seem, they are standard for executive profiles and probably realistic for the work itself. The old story about the presidential search committee at Yale University comes to mind. After failing to find a candidate who met their lofty expectations, one member of the committee came in with the enthusiastic report, "I have found the one who meets all of our expectations. There is only one question. Is God a Yale man?"

This same question applies to the "stunning opportunity" for the presidency in the profile above. Who can claim the personal maturity and professional competence to satisfy such a demanding range of expectations? Self-awareness, a key quality of effective leadership, comes into play. After going through the search process, the relative strengths and weaknesses of the elected leader are known to both the board and the individual. Knowing them, it is a serious error for the board to assume that its leader-to-be excels on all expectations. It is equally wrong to ignore any differences in strengths or weaknesses. To fulfill its responsibility for stewarding the resources of leadership, the board should call for a growth plan that begins with self-evaluation by the individual. It will be no threat to the person who is self-aware. Moreover, the relationship of trust it opens with the board that could be a life-saver in the long term.

Return to the list of expectations for the CEO in our sample profile. Assume, for instance, that the new CEO excels in vision casting but is weak in translating that vision into a strategic plan. What goal for growth is implied? Not all visionaries are planners and not all planners are implementers. If there is a weakness in any one of these steps, it should be addressed in a growth plan for the new leader. Now, extend the call for the CEO to be "champion of the vision, mission and core values" by modeling a contagious and maturing Christian faith. How is this expectation translated in a growth plan? Spiritual discipline is a continual process for any believer, particularly for one God calls to lead. Self-awareness itself will produce a goal for growth toward spiritual maturity.

"Where am I strong and where do I need to grow?" This is the question that a new CEO should be able to ask honestly and answer clearly. Strengths should be stated factually but humbly. Weaknesses should neither be glossed over nor presented as self-flagellation. The end result is a short list of growth goals based on self-awareness. The list includes progressive steps with measurable outcomes for personal and professional development.

Then, draw a dotted line between professional performance goals and personal growth goals for the CEO. Return one more time to the opportunity profile cited earlier (p. 144). "Strategic Planning" is identified as one of the primary roles of the CEO. A performance goal is implied. The expectation is that the CEO will do some strategic planning at some level of quality within some period of time. If, however, the CEO lacks knowledge or experience in strategic planning, a growth goal is also implied in the question, "How will it get done?" Performance goals and growth goals need to be seen as a dual responsibility for the board of a Christ-centered organization.

A Covenant Relationship

Once the initial growth plan has been completed, it should be presented as a discussion document to the board. The test of self-awareness shifts to the test of self-confidence. Is the CEO secure enough to be seen through the eyes of others? The board discussion prior to election of the CEO certainly included a review of strengths and weaknesses. This perspective should not remain hidden with the threat of future ambush. By being open and honest at the beginning, the board committee and CEO build a trust that sets the stage for all future assessments. So, as the board committee reviews the growth goals presented by the CEO, its members interact with revisions, deletions and additions. Their responsibility goes beyond critiquing the document. Where resources are needed for the growth goals, they should prepare recommendations in support of those resources. Together a mutual plan is forged for leadership development that will be reported to the whole board in executive session along with recommendations for funding and staffing as needed. The board now has in its hand evidence that nurturing the chief executive is part of its sacred trust.

With All Due Diligence
Board Check
Raising the Bar

Accepting its biblical responsibility for stewarding the leadership gifts of the CEO, our board has:

	Yes	No
1. specified "Nurturing the CEO" among the board duties stated in the by-laws;	_____	_____
2. identified in the board structure the point of responsibility for nurturing the CEO;	_____	_____
3. written the charge to the appropriate committee for nurturing the CEO;	_____	_____
4. identified the areas of personal and professional growth for CEO leadership;	_____	_____
5. distinguished the difference between performance goals and growth goals; and	_____	_____
6. mutually developed with our CEO a growth plan that is ready for implementation.	_____	_____

Chapter 18

Leading CEO Development
Compensating a Commitment

The job of CEO of a Christ-centered organization is demanding, stressful, and often exhausting. Neither money nor acclaim can match the rewards of answering God's call, doing God's will and serving God's people. Few leaders of Christ-centered organizations complain about their workload or whine about their pressures. Christian history is written in the lives of those who sacrificed themselves to serve others for the sake of Jesus Christ. If a common epitaph were written on their gravestones, it would read like the final words of the missionary who died alone on foreign shores: "No returns, no regrets, no reservations."

The willingness to sacrifice everything to answer God's call does not lift the burden from a board to conserve and cultivate the resources that run down with intensive use over time. In humans, one of these is energy. The first question a board should ask in the exhilarating moments of CEO election is, "How can we preserve the well-being of our gifted leader in the high-pressure job that we are asking him to do?" A close second is the more mundane challenge, "What economic freedom does our leader need to give full attention to the task?" On the heels of that question, still another comes to mind, "How can we assure the long-term security for our leader and family?" Only after these questions have been answered should the board address the need to protect the organization in the event of failure, dismissal or loss.

Even though the formal agreement between the board and its CEO will include financial, professional, administrative, and personal arrangements, the spirit of the relationship must be different. At one time, contractual agreements were almost unknown among Christ-centered organizations. A handshake, a prayer and a letter of appointment sealed a covenantal relationship. Today, it is not unusual to have a written contract with detailed stipulations ranging from negotiations on the initial salary to severance pay in the event of dismissal. While the good word of the board and the CEO is still involved, the letter of the law can take over as the primary means for enforcement. For Christ-centered organizations to get caught up in litigious thinking is a blight upon our witness.

We need to go back to the commitment of our sacred trust. Behind every word of agreement, by contract or by covenant, there is the common bond of our stewardship responsibility. We are responsible for resources—organizational and individual—that God has given to us. Being responsible, we are accountable to God for our stewardship of these resources. If there is any hint of an adversarial relationship between the board and the executive in the negotiations, stipulations, or enforcement of their agreement, the spirit of our sacred trust is lost. With great regret, I can remember case after case of bitter separation and litigious threats between boards and CEOs in Christ-centered organizations that were tried in the court of public media. Broken lives, lingering hate, and vengeful action followed. The world deserves better from us.

We have two goals, conserving the well-being of the individual and investing in the gift of leadership. So the board of a Christ-centered organization will consider financial, professional, administrative and personal agreements with its CEO are sealed by the spirit of our sacred trust.

Financial Agreements

Leaders of Christ-centered organizations are not in the ministry for money. These are not idle words. Almost without exception, those who lead our organizations are gifted far beyond their compensation. Some will leave lucrative positions to accept an appointment that requires the executive to fundraise his or her own salary. Others receive salaries that are marginal at best with minimal benefits for future security.

While avoiding the extremes, we need to make financial agreements with our leadership that assure the well-being of the person while on the job and for the future.

Salary. Many factors go into the decision that sets the salary of a executive. Starting with a living wage for the area where the ministry is located, factoring in the size and budget of the ministry, and then comparing salaries for similar ministries will give the board a range of options for consideration. Even more important is asking what salary level gives the leader economic freedom to do the job that the board asks? This guideline takes care of the lows that can cripple leadership and the highs that can spoil it.

Ratios between the salaries of the CEO, administrators, professional staff, and support staff can also be helpful. Although the ratios for ministries may differ—especially in fields where highly skilled professionals are involved—the working principle is that the CEO should never receive a salary that causes a gap in the economic level and takes sacrifice out of the position. Surveys of executive versus staff compensation will show the discrepancy. If the salary of the CEO is topping out the ranks while staff salaries are struggling against the average, something needs to be done. To ask professional peers to survive on economic margins while their leader has more than he needs is a fast track toward low morale and high turnover. In recent times, there have been instances where executive compensation in Christ-centered organizations followed the corporate trend of escalating salaries for the CEO. Following that pattern, some boards have added incentives and bonuses to reward and retain their executive leadership. Decisions like this contradict the meaning of commitment and sacrifice. Incentives for performance and retention bonuses have no place in the nonprofit Christ-centered organization.

Still, the salary of the leader should set the pace for the organization in its commitment to all its people's welfare. In one organization, a CEO who inherited wealth kept the salary scale depressed because he had no need for cost of living increases or merit pay. In another, a vice president refused to take an increase because she felt she already had enough to live on. Everyone below both of these leaders suffered. Guided by the Holy Spirit, common sense and practical wisdom balances the economic freedom needed by an executive leader to do the job without the extravagance of over-compensation or the depression of under-compensation.

Benefits. Compensation beyond the salary assures the present and future well-being of the executive leader. Comprehensive health insurance, medical and dental, should be provided to care for the individual and any immediate family members. Provision should also be made for annual physical examinations leading to a wellness plan that is essential for a person in a stressful job.

Life insurance, whether term or whole life and with matching contributions, is usually provided as part of the benefit package that applies to all employees of the organization. Key person insurance to cover accidental death while representing the ministry on the road deserves special consideration when the benefit is divided between the organization (to defray the cost of executive replacement) and the surviving spouse. Options, such as long-term care insurance, should be discussed as well.

Retirement plans go hand-in-hand with health insurance as a standard benefit in Christ-centered organizations. The board should take the lead in making a maximum contribution that the participant can match. Younger executives may prefer to have more salary during the years of raising a family, and those who are closer to retirement will want to maximize their contributions to retirement plans. The board will want to be sensitive to these differences. Even though executives of Christ-centered organizations will never float down into retirement on a golden parachute, the board can help assure a landing without disaster.

Professional Agreements

A CEO needs more than economic freedom to do the job. To be effective on the job and meet its performance expectations, the CEO needs full support of the board in specific areas of professional advancement.

Professional workshops. Every CEO has a need for professional development that is inseparable from personal growth. Whether in the initial agreement with its new CEO or after a regular assessment of its incumbent CEO, the board will encourage its leader to take advantage of seminars and workshops relating to professional skills and leadership development. They may advance the CEO's strength, improve an area of weakness or anticipate a new challenge for executive leadership. For instance, when the board and I recognized that the next level in institutional progress required a sound basis in strategic planning, I was given the opportunity to attend a week-long workshop led by an acknowledged expert in the field. The experience proved to be invaluable when I came home to lead the process with the confidence of a new skill. Strategic planning is only one area in which a CEO can gain competence. Depending upon institutional need and executive competence, seminars and workshops on administrative leadership, financial management, capital fundraising, board development and succession planning are examples of professional growth areas for CEOs that should be approved and funded by the board.

Professional leaves. As part of the board-CEO agreement, professional leaves ranging from sabbaticals lasting months and study leaves lasting weeks to special events lasting days should be included to affirm this kind of experience and avoid any misunderstanding.

Sabbaticals and study leaves are relatively new options for Christ-centered organizations, but when seen as part of our stewardship responsibility, they can serve as opportunities for recreating the energy and developing the gifts of our chief executive while advancing our mission.

More will be said about the sabbatical concept in chapter 20. For now, our purpose is to see it as part of the total compensation package for the CEO. Because the average tenure for CEOs continues to be in the five-year range, this period of time is often used to qualify a CEO for the leave. Also, after five years of intensive work on a 24/7 basis, most CEOs come to the time when they have put their vision into place with established programs so that both the CEO and the organization need either a change or a break. The board should be reading these signs, not just after five years of service, but along the way.

In one case, the board of a Christ-centered organization learned that their CEO could go full charge for a couple of years and then slump into exhaustion. The board, therefore, sent him and his wife to a family ranch in the Southwest for six weeks of creative renewal without counting the time against either vacation or sabbatical time.

In another case, a "honeymoon break" for a get-away weekend was funded by the board during a energy-draining capital campaign for a highly successful CEO and his wife.

Sensitivity to individual differences can prevent stagnation or burnout. A provision for a professional leave written into the board-CEO agreement seals the commitment of the board to grow its leader and gives incentive for the CEO to work with full intensity. In turn, a sabbatical plan submitted by a CEO and approved by the board should include a proposed project for professional development, a time schedule, a budget to fund the proposal, and a plan for executive delegation during the time of absence. Not infrequently, a sabbatical provision will include some obligation for the CEO to continue with the organization after returning from leave or arrange appropriate remuneration for the cost of the experience. The emphasis, however, should be upon the opportunity for professional advancement. Whatever it takes to refresh and revitalize the CEO is worthwhile.

Professional expenses. A contractual provision for job-related expenses may seem mundane, but they again send the signal that the board understands the role of its leader. Travel, auto, conference, and entertainment expenses should be fully reimbursed as well as membership fees for professional associations and civic or community clubs that are relevant to the mission of the organization and the work of its leader. Delicate questions often arise at this latter point because the perception of some memberships, such as country clubs, can be distorted in the public mind or in the view of the organization's staff and stakeholders. To err on the side of caution, the board should avoid running away from the constituency and listen to the voice of the Spirit in making such decisions.

Personal Agreements

Nothing is more important to the board of a Christ-centered organization than to have the leader's spouse and family in sync with the mission of the ministry. Tragic stories have been written about leaders who neglected their families for the sake of their ministry. In one case, the daughter of a bishop said, "I remember every birthday because my daddy wasn't home." Another daughter of the leader of an international organization voiced similar despair when she called her father to say, "Daddy, if I were an orphan, you would remember it was my birthday."

We dare not forget that spouses and families also make sacrifices so that a leader can answer the call of God. Board members of Christ-centered organizations are overseers for the relationships, especially in encouraging a balance between faith and family, home and work. At the baseline, moving expenses should be provided. If the executive qualifies for clergy status in the eyes of the IRS, a minister's housing allowance should be approved.

Vacation time is one of the key indicators of the CEO's ability to relax, refresh and give full attention to the family. Three weeks should be the minimum with additional time added based on service. Limiting accumulated vacation time encourages the reluctant CEO to get away and also avoids awkward negotiations at the time of resignation or retirement. Executives should also be encouraged to take their vacation in large chunks of time and not call the office every other day. Most executives admit that it takes at least three days to wind down from office pressures and another three days to gear up for the return. That means a week at a time is effectively only one day of vacation. Families that sacrifice time together during the year deserve a vacation scheduled for two weeks or more.

No copy-and-paste template can be recommended for the compensation agreement between the board and its CEO. After working through the basics of financial, professional and personal support, the board must ask whether or not the compensation matches the expectations for the role and for the fulfillment of the mission. Then and only then can it take the next step of stretching the gifts of their leader toward their full potential.

With All Due Diligence
Board Check
Compensating a Commitment

In support for the personal and professional well-being of our CEO, our board has:

	Yes	No
1. provided a compensation package that gives our CEO the economic freedom needed to do the job we expect;	_____	_____
2. assured benefits that give long-term security to our CEO and immediate family;	_____	_____
3. written an agreement that goes beyond a legal contract to a relational covenant;	_____	_____
4. offered a salary that is:		
a. comparable to other Christ-centered organizations in the same sector,	_____	_____
b. balanced in ratio with other salaries within the organization;	_____	_____
5. included in the agreement such provisions as:		
a. health examinations,	_____	_____
b. health insurance,	_____	_____
c. life insurance,	_____	_____
d. key person insurance,	_____	_____

e. retirement plan,   _____   _____

f. housing,   _____   _____

g. vacation time,   _____   _____

h. sabbatical time,   _____   _____

i. professional expenses,   _____   _____

j. entertainment expenses,   _____   _____

k. professional memberships,   _____   _____

l. other _____; and   _____   _____

6. clarified by agreement such
   administrative details as:

a. starting date,   _____   _____

b. term of office,   _____   _____

c. performance evaluation schedule, and   _____   _____

d. termination and severance provisions.   _____   _____

Chapter 19

Leading CEO Development Partnering in Confidence

Nurturing a CEO goes beyond assuring a measure of economic freedom to do a demanding job and providing for personal and family renewal. To fulfill its sacred trust, the board of a Christ-centered organization also is responsible for personal and professional growth at every level. Supporting a climate of growth is how the board shows its continuing commitment to the CEO. Here is where relational, intellectual, and spiritual resources become part of the growth plan for nurturing its leader. While the leader is primarily responsible for his or her own growth, the self-aware CEO will anticipate needs and opportunities for relational, intellectual, and spiritual growth while in executive office. At this point, the board's responsibility is to encourage, support and, if necessary, resource these personal interests in improvement. But the responsibility does not stop there. There are intersections in the board-executive relationship where the board becomes an active partner in stretching its leader to full potential.

Board-CEO Relationship

CEO development is all about relationships. At the very center of this truth is the relationship between the board and its CEO. Every other aspect of CEO development depends upon the quality of this relationship. Sooner or later, an issue will arise or a decision will be made that determines the depth of commitment, strains goodwill, and tests the bond of trust. If the board-CEO bond is strong, there is a climate of mutual learning and growth. If the bond of trust is frayed or broken, however, it is seldom repaired. Even where forgiveness and reconciliation are integral to the character of the ministry, a break in the line of trust is rarely restored. Not enough can be said about the importance of unconditional trust between the board and its CEO. Trust is the basis for a pervasive climate of learning and growth throughout the organization. Out of unconditional trust, then, the board confidently empowers the CEO and the CEO willingly engages the board as a partner in the ministry.

Trust takes time. In bare-boned terms, the board is the owner of the Christ-centered organization and the CEO is its sole employee. Even in a relationship of mutual trust, the formal lines of authority and accountability cannot be violated. If this relationship is tested, a simple rule prevails: *In a contest between the board and the CEO, the board always wins.* One of the growth goals for a leader is to learn to work with a higher authority. In the search of a CEO, we look for leaders who are visionary, creative, and strong willed self-starters. These gifts, however, must be directed and disciplined within the context of organizational structures and varying relationships with the board itself. At one extreme are highly successful ministries headed by charismatic leaders who hold authority and accountability in their own hands or have a hand-picked board to confirm their personal policies and practices. Entrepreneurial founders of exploding ministries have the hardest time making the adjustment from a personalized operation to an administrative structure with someone else being executive. In such cases, a CEO never has a chance to grow because the founder is always second-guessing decisions and stifling creativity. At the other extreme are Christ-centered organizations where a dominating board dictates passive CEO leadership.

Either extreme falls far short of our sacred trust. Dare we envision a strong board and a strong leader in the same setting? One board member said, "We have a choice, either a strong board and weak executive or a weak board and a strong executive." Is this the only alternative? Can we not expect to find mission compatibility and a mutual trust in which the board empowers the CEO and the CEO engages the board without exterior motives? Thankfully, my lasting impressions of board-CEO relationships in Christ-centered organizations is positive. Each party may have it flaws, but they are never fatal when the motive is to do the good will of God. Because the Holy Spirit works best with feet of clay, we have hope. So many times, I have witnessed a floundering board struggle with a conflicted leadership and come to a redemptive outcome. To accomplish this goal, two-way communication, collegiality, counsel, and confidence must be active. This is the climate in which the board and its CEO learn and grow together.

Earlier, we asked the question "What does the board owe its CEO?" Our answer: (a) the board's responsibility to set the policy to be implemented by executive action, (b) give the support that sets the CEO free to fulfill the board's expectations, (c) serve as an objective source for reviewing and critiquing executive proposals, (d) offer counsel for personal and professional growth, and (e) be a friend and a brother, especially in times of stress. We also need to ask, "What does the CEO owe the board?" The most obvious answer is to (1) acknowledge its authority, (2) assure personal integrity, (3) accept its counsel, (4) achieve performance expectations, and (5) lead by vision and planning.

There is more. In a climate of learning and growing together, the CEO of a Christ-centered organization sees the board members as more than legal functionaries. They are colleagues, friends, brothers and sisters who learn and grow together for the greater good of the Kingdom of God. Active CEOs, however, are so overwhelmed by their executive tasks that they seldom have the time required to build the board. Retired CEOs have a different story. When asked what they would do differently, they most often say, "I would give more time to developing the board." There is good reason for this response. The board that a CEO leaves behind is a legacy that can impel or impede the success of the leader who follows. Board development and CEO nurture go hand in hand.

The Pivotal CEO/Chair Partnership

The key indicator for a nurturing climate in a Christ-centered organization is the relationship between the board chair and the CEO. Moments ago, we described a healthy relationship between the board and its CEO as one that is characterized by communication, collegiality, counsel, and confidence. Now, we can say with assurance that these qualities turn on the pivot of the partnership between board chair and CEO. In fact, if you want to read the health of a Christ-centered organization, the success of a CEO, and the vitality of its board, find out how the board chair and CEO relate to each other. There is instance after instance of board conflict and CEO failure when that line is broken or frayed. The relationship begins during the search process when the board chair: (a) becomes a major contact with the candidate; (b) continues through negotiations related to the position; (c) formalizes the election of the CEO; (d) interacts on policies and programs; (e) undergoes testing in times of crisis: (f) and matures with the CEO in a mutual vision for the future of the ministry. None of this happens at once. Forged over time in the crucible of leadership, the board chair-CEO relationship is at the very heart of a ministry where people learn and grow.

The starting point is *an unconditional line of trust.* The quality of trust between the board chair and CEO in a Christ-centered ministry sets the tone for whole organization. In one instance, the board chair and I disagreed. When I explained my decision to him, he said, "Even though I do not fully agree, I trust your decision as our chief executive." In another case, I disagreed with the outcome of a board meeting and nuanced that in my report to the staff of the organization. Immediately, word went through the filter of other minds who disagreed with the board's decision. Equally fast, word reached the chair about the interpretation. He called me in, took me to the woodshed, and trust was restored when I recanted. In still another incident, I failed to report a violation of policy by a vice president to the board chair because I felt I could handle it myself. Another vice president, however, reported the violation to the board chair and ignited a firestorm of undercover investigation. It concluded with my innocence, but at the expense of our relationship. An unconditional line of trust was never fully restored. In each case, I grew by acknowledging my part in the problem and learning how to work with my board chair.

Closely related to the line of unconditional trust between board chair and CEO is *confidential communication of needs.* However you cut it, CEO leadership is a lonely job and no one understands what it means to be in the position unless they have been there. CEO development begins in the final interview with the search committee when gifts of leadership are weighed against weaknesses that need to be strengthened. In final negotiations with the candidate, the board chair has a responsibility to talk about these expectations and lay the groundwork for a CEO growth plan. With new CEOs, this often begins with a board-funded workshop in the field of management. From then on, the board chair and CEO will be in regular communication—more than an information session about the status of the ministry. As a board chair of three Christ-centered organizations, I regularly asked the CEO my favorite question, "What is it that keeps you awake at night?" I also took it upon myself to pay attention to the cues of overwork, excessive stress, health problems, relational conflicts, spiritual depression, and neglect of family.

In the Christ-centered organization we can expect the board chair-CEO relationship to go beyond the line connecting a superior with a subordinate. Far deeper than that formal connection is the covenant relationship between members of the Body of Christ and a common commitment to the ministry. At the same time, we cannot escape the fact that the board chair represents the authority of the board to whom the CEO is accountable.

On the professional side of the board chair-CEO relationship, we come to the value of *a leadership team for processing proposals and recommendations that will go to the full board.* Good governance requires careful preparation of executive plans for policies, programs and people in the ministry. A key checkpoint along the way is the meeting of minds between the board chair and the CEO. Prior to board meetings, the board chair and CEO work together on an agenda that will set priorities to give maximum time and attention to policy-related matters. If the board chair and the CEO disagree on a recommendation, the differences should be ironed out in private session so that they will come to the board in agreement. Threat of disaster hangs over any board session where the board chair and the CEO take conflicting positions. In one case, a CEO had carefully prepared a finely-tuned and balanced budget based upon available resources. During the meeting of the finance committee, the CEO was called out to another committee, and the board chair went along with a recommendation to increase staff salaries across the board, throwing the budget out of balance. The board chair expected the CEO to raise funds for the difference. Crisis ensued in the open session. The CEO had to restate the case for the original budget recommendation and lay his leadership on the line. The full board finally backed down and supported the CEO, but not without the loss of valuable time and unnecessary conflict. If the board chair and the CEO had come together on the budget recommendation prior to the meeting, the crisis would have been avoided. As always, such a situation is a time for learning and growing, not just for the CEO, but for the board chair as well.

The quality of the board chair-CEO relationship also comes into play in the *assessment cycle of executive leadership.* Initially, the board chair invites the CEO to prepare personal growth goals as well as professional performance standards. In private session, then, they work and rework until both agree that these are the outcomes on which the CEO will be assessed. When presented to executive committee or the full board, the chair and CEO stand as one. As the cycle of assessment then turns with annual reviews and periodic formal surveys, it is the board chair who has the responsibility to communicate the results and work with the CEO on strengths and weaknesses. Unless they have been growing together, honest assessment can be a serious threat, debilitating rather than developmental. There is no substitute for an ongoing relationship in which the board chair and CEO grow together.

Assessing Our Efficiency

Why all of this emphasis upon the board chair and CEO as a leadership team? As stated, a commitment to CEO development cannot be separated from a nurturing climate that involves every member of the Christ-centered organization. It begins with the relationship between the board chair and the CEO. Maturity in this relationship sets the tone of interaction throughout the whole organization. Having answered these questions for themselves, the board chair and CEO can now challenge the board with the same questions.

- Are we board members in response to the call of God?

- Are we unified in spirit on the mission of our ministry?

- Are we working together in a climate of trust?

- Are we able to handle conflict and come to reconciliation?

- Are we keeping the pledge of confidence for sensitive matters?

- Are we learning and growing together?

- Are we finding our trusteeship spiritually meaningful and personally rewarding?

An astute observer will note the parallel between these questions and the relationship between the board chair and CEO. Every member of a Christ-centered organization, whether board chair, board member, CEO or staff, is entrusted with the responsibility for stewardship that exercises the same principles and works with the same spirit. A *commitment* to each other, *confidence* in each other, *communication* with each other, and *counsel* for each other are the ingredients for a sense of *community* in a Christ-centered organization where all members can learn and grow.

With All Due Diligence
Board Check
Partnering in Confidence

To confirm the partnership between our board and our CEO, we have:

	Yes	No
1. a bond of total trust between us;	_____	_____
2. open and two-way lines of communication;	_____	_____
3. collegial interaction in board and committee sessions;	_____	_____
4. a strong and unified leadership team in our board chair and our CEO;	_____	_____
5. a mutual commitment between our board chair and our CEO for executive development:	_____	_____
a. an unconditional line of trust,	_____	_____
b. confidential communication of needs,	_____	_____
c. a unified plan for CEO growth,	_____	_____
d. unified presentation of proposals,	_____	_____
e. objective assessment of CEO leadership; and	_____	_____
6. a board that qualifies as a learning organization, an organic community, and spiritual body.	_____	_____

Chapter 20

Leading CEO Development Pushing the Envelope

L eadership is an expandable resource. Most boards of Christ-centered organizations have done a good job of supporting the CEO through compensation and benefits that give the freedom and security needed to do a strenuous job. More boards are taking on the responsibility for nurturing a climate in which board, CEO, and staff grow together in their relationships and their work. Fewer boards have seen stretching the CEO as part of their nurturing role, especially when it comes to the stretch of moral, intellectual and spiritual resources. They assume these are personal matters and the responsibility of the individual. While this assumption is basically true, the board can encourage development in these areas through the benefits for an executive who is morally alert, intellectually awake, and spiritually alive.

The Moral Stretch

Most of the work of CEOs of Christ-centered organizations is routine—staff meetings, office appointments, answering mail, conference calls, public speaking, and fundraising. Every once in a while, however, that routine is punctuated by a crisis that stretches the leader because it is more than a management challenge; it is a moral choice. In management parlance, such an event is called a "critical incident."[1] The term defines itself

[1] J. C. Flanagan, *The Critical Incident Technique*, Psychological Bulletin, 1954, 51, 327-358.

by: (a) *unexpected circumstances* that are also unprecedented; (b) *personal conflict* that is emotionally intense; (c) *moral choice* that is neither black nor white; and (d) *long-term consequences* that determine the destiny of leadership. Although a critical incident of these proportions might be unusual, no CEO is exempt from them. For example, a Christ-centered organization that hires only committed Christians may be challenged by a civic ordinance that prohibits religious discrimination. Or an employee may be caught in a scandal that can rock the public image of the ministry. Or again, a prospective donor may attach strings to a major gift that will undercut the primary mission of the organization. Every leader of a Christ-centered organization can add to the list.

In times like these, the board must show confidence in its executive leader with counsel and encouragement but not by interference or second-guessing. When the moral choice must be made in a grey area and pragmatic compromise is part of the decision, failure is a possibility. This will stretch the bond of trust between the board and its CEO. Board members have to remember that an executive learns best while on the job dealing with real-time situations. Rather than condemning a decision, the board should ask, "What did we learn from it?" Unless there is a breach of integrity or policy, a critical incident is a white-hot crucible in which leaders are refined by fire and shaped for service.

The Intellectual Stretch

In the creation account, God created the Sabbath on the seventh day when He rested from His work. Later, He instructed the Israelites to give their fields a "Sabbath" every seventh year by letting the soil lie fallow to restore the nutrients needed for growing healthy crops. The academic community has led the way by picking up this biblical principle and giving faculty members a sabbatical every seventh year of their tenure. Why not bring the same principle of personal renewal to our CEOs in Christ-centered organizations?

At one time, anyone in ministry, whether clergy or laity, was expected to "burn out" rather than "rust out." This attitude is no better than the secular idea of hiring chief executives, exhausting their resources, and floating them into retirement on a golden parachute. It assumes that leadership is expendable rather than a resource to be conserved. Therefore, it contradicts the concept of the Sabbath. If the board of a Christ-centered organization is faithful to its sacred trust, we will find a way to renew the energy and expand the potential of our executive leader.

As noted earlier, sabbaticals are relatively new to executives of Christ-centered organizations, but leadership can be recycled, renewed, and expanded for the good of the person and of the organization.

The purpose of a sabbatical is more than renewal of expendable energy; it is an investment in the potential of the individual and in the future of the Christ-centered ministry. Every executive leader is a person of many gifts and many interests. When a person assumes leadership, he makes priorities for time and energy and some of those gifts or interests have to be put aside. One CEO of a Christ-centered organization said, "When I was elected president, I had to abandon my research and writing for a book on theology." Another mentioned deferring the life-long dream of an extended trip following in the footsteps of the Apostle Paul. Still another felt limited in the time available to pursue a blossoming reputation as an artist depicting Christian history. Each of these interests is like a gleam in the eye. Ask any executive leader, "What would you like to do if you had the time?" Watch for the gleam and you will discover the ray of renewal.

Sabbaticals are different than vacations. A vacation is used primarily for physical and mental renewal. A sabbatical, however, should be a "stretch" time when the leader is refreshed by exploration on the growing edge of individual interest with benefit for the future of the organization. Sabbatical time will vary from organization to organization though six months in the standard range. A sabbatical plan submitted by the CEO and approved by the board includes a proposal, time schedule, and budget for the project as well as administrative arrangements for the time of absence. Samples of actual sabbatical projects for a leader include:

- writing a book from insights in a daily journal;

- reading primary sources in the history of the theology behind the organization's statement of faith;

- taking classes to understand the new technology;

- visiting other chief executives to learn from them;

- catching up on heavy reading and bringing back the ten best books for the staff;

- creating a portfolio of artistic line drawings of historic places;

- attending an advanced school of management; and

- driving a taxicab to understand a changing culture.

Imagine what each of these CEOs brought back to their organization—a book written, a unique travel experience, an art form cultivated, an expansive reading developed, or a professional skill mastered. The gleam will be renewed and the incentive for personal improvement will be contagious.

As an extra benefit of a CEO sabbatical, it serves as an in-depth test of executive leadership. Having to delegate CEO responsibility to a second-in-command, the chief executive reveals whether or not—and how—subordinates are being groomed. In one case, this advantage was lost when the chief executive called back every other day to make sure things were on track. In another case, a CEO left on a sabbatical with full confidence in the skills of the executive vice president whom he had groomed. Six weeks later, he had to cut short the sabbatical and return home to quell a major crisis. Later, a consultant used the analogy of an airplane pilot to tell what had gone wrong. He said the executive vice president was well-prepared to handle the organization while on a routine flight but had no experience in dealing with a crash landing. Every sabbatical is a teaching experience for the CEO, the board, and the whole organization.

The Spiritual Stretch

Continuing growth toward spiritual maturity is a natural expectation for the CEO of a Christ-centered organization. Evidence of spiritual maturity is always at the top of the list of qualifications in the Leadership Profile. A search committee needs to hear the candidate give personal witness to a spiritual journey with the promise of continuing progress. Questions about active participation in a local church, Bible studies, and growth groups are often asked along with interest in personal devotions and spiritual discipline. Upon election, however, the inquiry stops and it is expected that the individual will progress spiritually in the leadership role. Experience says that we may expect too much. CEOs who are constantly on the run find it hard to stop and become thoroughly engaged in the life of the local church, meet the weekly expectations of a Bible study session, attend an accountability group or set aside daily time for solitude and spiritual reflection. For this reason, the personal growth plan of the CEO should include some self-initiated benchmarks for spiritual development leading toward the goal foreseen by the Apostle Paul in II Timothy 3:17, "…so that the man (or woman) of God may be thoroughly equipped for every good work."

A CEO who is serious about spiritual growth may well invite the board to partner in this plan as a checkpoint along the way. As part of the regular evaluation schedule, the board might ask about the executive's engagement in a worshipping congregation. Because participation in a confessing and forgiving community of faith requires a vulnerability that runs counter to the public image, a chief executive may find it hard to participate fully. Bible studies may be less threatening, but again the leader can be put in an awkward position when the members expect him or her to have all of the answers. Still, because the board expects that its executive leader is growing in the Word, it can request the CEO lead devotions regularly throughout the year as a checkpoint on new insights and applications for personal or corporate Bible study.

Cell groups dedicated to spiritual development with an emphasis upon personal accountability may well be a part of a CEO's growth plan. When these groups are made up of persons who are either accountable to the CEO or have a vested interest in the ministry of the Christ-centered organization, their value is decreased. Because CEOs occupy lonely positions with conflicts and temptations unique to their role, they need a spiritual confidant with whom they can share their deepest thoughts and most dangerous feelings. Objectivity and confidentiality are the criteria for this relationship. Whether with a group of friends or a mentor, a leader must be assured of complete confidence and be willing to let the truth be spoken in love. The spiritual stretch will come as the relationship deepens and the God-breathed Word "… is useful for teaching, rebuking, correcting and training in righteousness."

Threads of support, partnership, and stretch are now interwoven in the responsibility of the board for nurturing CEO leadership. The task is not onerous because the outcomes are so rewarding. When a board honors its sacred trust for the stewardship of leadership resources, an environment conducive to professional and personal growth is created for all members of the Christ-centered organization. Work is meaningful, goals are reached, and God gets the glory.

With All Due Diligence
Board Check
Pushing the Envelope

Recognizing that our CEO will grow by being stretched, our board has:

	Yes	No
1. created a climate that encourages our CEO to take creative risks, make bold decisions, and even "go against the grain" at times;	_____	_____
2. supported our CEO's hard decisions in morally ambiguous circumstances;	_____	_____
3. asked "What did we learn from it?" when risk-taking did not produce the expected results or even led to failure;	_____	_____
4. encouraged intentional intellectual growth for our CEO; and	_____	_____
5. entered into a covenant with our CEO for mutual spiritual growth and accountability.	_____	_____

Chapter 21

Leading CEO Development Measuring Wholeness

Assessment is a word that conjures up a host of negative images. Whether leftover from final exams in school or physical examinations with the doctor, we dislike the thought and avoid the fact. Perhaps this explains why boards of Christ-centered organizations are reluctant to make assessment a priority and CEOs are glad to forget about it. Our sacred trust, however, makes assessment an integral part of CEO nurture. Just as benchmarks must have a follow-up process to be effective, goals for growth—whether personal or professional—must have assessment in order to complete the cycle of CEO leadership. As the executive is accountable to the board for working the plan, the board is accountable to the executive for assuring the process. Mutual accountability with the promise of positive outcomes shifts our attitude from a management nuisance to a governance principle. As stewards of the trust, we do not know if our support for the CEO, partnership with the CEO, and stretching of the CEO are effective until we assess the outcomes.

What Do We Assess?

The professional performance of the CEO is based on criteria stated or implied in the primary documents guiding governance. As always, the mission statement comes first. When all is said and done, the final question for CEO performance is, "Has our mission advanced on your watch?" Close behind this question are the goals of the strategic plan. Urgent goals must be met, intermediate goals must be in process, and long-range goals must be in view. Within the

177

larger framework of this larger strategy, there will be tactical goals for divisions or departments that test the CEO's ability to delegate authority and trust the executive team.

Mission statement, strategic plan and tactical delegation comprise the background for CEO assessment. The job description itself is the pinchpoint. When the search process is organized around the Leadership Profile for the CEO with qualifications and priorities, the expectations are readily translated into performance goals for ongoing assessment. For instance, if the Profile puts priority on turn-around management for the ministry, a clear and measurable goal comes into view. From the Profile, then, the CEO adopts a set of manageable goals that form the content for an annual "State of the Union" address to the board and the members of the organization. This address will have an intimacy of communication and commitment that bonds the board, CEO, and staff in common cause. Rather than just citing facts and figures about the status of the organization, the annual address should be a self-assessment of progress toward the performance goals for which the executive was hired. Facts and figures support achievements and form the basis for projected goals for the year ahead. A board will be able to review this annual report not as an isolated document but as a means for assessing performance against expectations then and work with the CEO on common goals for future performance. A CEO has to be secure in the position in order to announce goals for the year ahead. Even more security is needed for the CEO to come back to the board and staff with a self-assessment at the end of the year. Yet there is no better way to model a climate of assessment for all members of the organization, including the board, that is open, honest and affirmative.

How Do We Assess?

Instruments for executive assessment range from standard forms to customized editions. A board may engage outside consultants for this special purpose. Objectivity is the value of an external assessment, but so often at the sacrifice of understanding the history, theology, ethos and spirit of the organization. Besides, if the mission statement, strategic plan and Leadership Profile written clearly and precisely, the board already has the best resource for CEO assessment. The board chair, the committee facilitating the assessment, and the CEO together can produce the most effective instrument for doing a quality job.

The key to creating an instrument for assessment is to stick with the Leadership Profile, making sure that the evaluation criteria are as objective as possible. No assessment based on hidden, fuzzy, or personalized criteria should ever take place. Whether it is the board in an executive session for annual review or a formal evaluation conducted among all members of the organization, the assessment should judge performance against mutually agreed upon goals. For instance, the introduction to a survey might read:

> The following goals for CEO performance were mutually agreed upon by our board and our CEO. We invite you to complete the following evaluation of our CEO based on these goals. Indicate the extent to which you believe the goals were achieved and give examples to support your answer. Feel free to extend your comments. Your signature is optional. All responses will be held in confidence.

The purpose of this statement is to reduce the chance that CEO assessment will become a popularity contest based on personality. Those who want to vent their emotions or plead their case are given the opportunity if they wish to use the back of the form, but when this happens, those who interpret the results can filter the comments to avoid excessive praise or criticism. Whatever the instrument, it should be read with objectivity and simplicity in mind. Expectations for professional performance should be professionally assessed.

Executive assessment in a Christ-centered organization may baffle board members accustomed to a single criterion: the "bottom line" of a balance sheet, a membership growth chart, a conversion rate, or funding goals. Ministry always involves intangibles that cannot be measured in numbers. How do we measure spiritual growth in a CEO? Assume, for instance, that the spiritual growth plan includes "increased sensitivity to the needs of others," "becoming a better listener," or "becoming a better student of the Word." Here is where the 360-degree review checks in. By asking superiors, peers, and subordinates to appraise their CEO, a spiritual growth perspective comes into view showing agreements as well as disagreements. The results may be affirming or painful, but, in either case, the groundwork is laid for continuing spiritual growth.

When the board gives the results of the appraisal, a general statement is best. The board has already given its word that assessments will be confidential and used for CEO development. It need only quash assumptions that the executive is in trouble, but need not make public any specific results. Professional people will understand and agree.

When Do We Assess?

CEO leadership assessment is a cyclical process. After the original appointment, the annual review begins. Because the first year of a CEO's tenure is so pivotal to future success, it is good for the board to schedule a time in executive session for the members to talk with the CEO present and alone without the CEO. The board chair's job is to keep these sessions objective and positive. Having developed a relationship with the CEO, there should be no secrets or surprises that come out of the meeting that the board chair has not shared or cannot share with a colleague. The same plan for executive sessions, with and without the CEO, should be on the agenda of every annual meeting.

A more formal evaluation is done after the first term of office, most often on three- or five-year cycle. Unless the assessment cycle is built into the contractual agreement, it is usually the CEO who takes the initiative. This is the time to survey the staff and selected members of the constituency (such as major givers). An outside consultant may be used. The survey can be one page divided into three parts: (a) rating of CEO performance according to the priority goals in the Leadership Profile; (b) projection of priorities for CEO leadership in the next three- to five-years; and (c) recommendations for areas of CEO growth to improve future performance. Respondents are asked for their perceptions in each of these areas. The same confidentiality and exclusive board use are made clear.

After reviewing the results of the formal survey, discussing them in executive session with the board, and having the board chair summarize the findings with the CEO, the assessment may be used to extend the contractual agreement for another term in office. An alternative is to put in place a "rolling contract" whereby the term of office is rolled forward another year after each successful annual review. Of course, the assessment may also be used to renegotiate the contract with appropriate increases in salary and benefits according to changing needs.

Thus the cycle of assessment begins with the performance expectations of the Leadership Profile, touches down in annual reviews at executive sessions of the board, advances to formal assessment on a three- to five-year schedule, and has continuity in the personalized relationship between the board chair and the CEO. The cycle turns again and again with longevity in office.

Why Assessment?

CEO leadership assessment consumes time and energy. Board members of Christ-centered organizations may question its value when there are so many other things that need to be done. Rather than taking a systematic approach to assessment, it is easier to do it "hit-or-miss" or not at all when the ministry is riding on the high tide of effective leadership. The fact is that the discipline of assessment may be more important in good times because it may too late in bad times. Warren Buffet, a secular and intriguing curmudgeon, nailed the truth when he mused, "Until the tide goes out, you never know who's swimming naked." One board of an international missions program had a large majority of corporate leaders for its membership. Out of their experience, they resisted the idea of executive assessment during start-up years when the organization flourished under the vision of its founder. At one meeting, however, some disgruntled board members called for an executive session because the founder's leadership style did not keep pace with the burgeoning growth of the organization. Red flags flew throughout the organization when the executive staff was dismissed from the meeting. The ministry never fully recovered because the relationship between the CEO and the board became clouded with doubt and suspicion. A prior commitment to the cycle of assessment might not have saved the ministry in the long run, but a mutually-developed growth plan might have addressed his weaknesses. Good stewardship calls for assessment with these principles in mind.

Assessment is our biblical principle. The creation account in Genesis is not complete until we read that God stopped His work at the end of each day, assessed His progress, and pronounced it "Good." At the end of the seventh day, when His work was complete and He rested, He also looked over the whole of creation and exclaimed, "It is very good!" On-going systematic assessment with reflection on the big picture is more than an option for the board of a Christ-centered organization. It is the model given to us by God Himself.

Assessment completes the cycle of our sacred trust. A board that recognizes leadership as a rare gift for which it is responsible will support the well-being of the person, become a partner in mutual trust, and find the growing edge for stretching leadership to its full potential. This is not enough. The cycle is not complete until assessment resets the benchmarks upon which personal, professional, and spiritual growth is based. A board that includes assessment in its portfolio gives stewardship its best meaning.

182

Assessment creates a climate for accountability. A culture of entitlement can carry over into the Christ-centered organization. Even without labor unions, underlying suspicion divides management and labor. Some units of the organization may send the signal that they feel superior to others. Some individuals may assume that they are responsible only to God. Each of these underlying ills is countered by a board and CEO that open themselves to peer review and performance assessment. Change, however, comes hard. Even when the CEO becomes a model for assessment and its attendant values, some will say that he or she is an exception. Yet if the Christ-centered organization is to learn and grow, the board and CEO must make a commitment to assessment, model its benefits, and regularize the process throughout the organization. In a societal culture of entitlement, accountability leading toward personal, professional, and spiritual maturity is a bright edge for our Christian witness.

With All Due Diligence
Board Check
Measuring Wholeness

Acknowledging that assessment is the step that completes the cycle of presidential nurture, our board:

	Yes	No
1. includes "assessment of the CEO" as part of our formal duties;	_____	_____
2. adopts performance goals for our CEO with assessable outcomes;	_____	_____
3. evaluates our CEO on such critical factors as:		
a. advancing the mission,	_____	_____
b. achieving strategic goals,	_____	_____
c. overseeing tactical outcomes;	_____	_____
4. reviews the annual report of the CEO as self-assessment for:		
a. achieving performance goals,	_____	_____
b. acknowledging areas of need;	_____	_____
5. plans a schedule for CEO assessment, such as:		
a. annual review by the board in executive session,	_____	_____

b. formal term review, including
   members of the organization,   _____   _____

c. professional review by outside
   consultant;   _____   _____

6. uses CEO assessment to promote the
   policy of accountability throughout
   the organization; and   _____   _____

7. communicates the policy of CEO
   assessment within the context
   of biblical accountability.   _____   _____

Chapter 22

Leading CEO Development
A Maturing Model

R uth Graham humbles us when she suggested that the sign over her life should read, "Under construction. Please be patient." The words apply particularly to CEOs of Christ-centered organizations. Even though the expectations posted in the Leadership Profile tend to be idealistic, real time experience tells us that there is always room for growth. Good and great leaders are always under construction and our boards must make patience a part of nurture.

What are the characteristics of mature Christian leadership? The final answer depends upon needs and expectations at a given point in time, but are there characteristics that apply to all Christian leaders wherever they are? Earlier, we referred to Paul's letter to Timothy where he wrote:

> All Scripture is given God-breathed and is useful
> for teaching, rebuking, correcting and instruction
> in righteousness, so that the man of God may be
> thoroughly equipped for every good work.
> II Timothy 3:16-17

Within these words board members will find a teaching-learning process for Christian leadership that the most experienced educator will envy. On the teaching side is the content of Scripture, the instruction of the Holy Spirit, and the lessons of experience through teaching, rebuking, correcting and instructing in righteousness. The outcomes of this learning are equally clear, a whole man or woman of God thoroughly equipped for every good work. Most remarkable is the fact that the teaching-learning process is wrapped in a holistic approach found in the words, "*All* Scripture," "the man of God," "*thoroughly* equipped," "for *every* good work." The "man of God" is taken to mean the *whole* man of God, and it is in these emphasized words, we see a level of maturity that is the goal for personal and professional development in every Christian. This is especially true for those called to lead our organizations and ministries. From this scripture we see the characteristics of a maturing model of Christian leadership.

The Lifetime Learner

Learning in truth. Board members of a Christ-centered organization expect that their executive leader will be a student of all Scripture, whether or not the person is theologically educated. The fully inspired Word of God is the final word for our faith and conduct— and more. We depend upon revealed truth for the principles that define and distinguish the character of our leadership. Daily insights from the Word provide a background for administrative decisions. In-depth searches in the whole of Scripture create the lens through which to cast a vision or design a strategy. Retreating to study the Word in times of personal stress and organizational conflict leads to inner peace and relational reconciliation. For a student of the Word, maturing in truth is a natural process that will be seen in its impact upon the text and tone of leadership. Board members of Christ-centered organizations will have no trouble seeing the signs of their CEO maturing in truth. As suggested earlier, regular devotionals messages given by the CEO are opportunities for sharing the insights that are the basis for principled leadership.

Learning in spirit. In Scripture that is God-breathed, we feel the pulsating presence of the Holy Spirit giving life to every part of the whole. He is the One Jesus said would walk along beside us to "convict the world of guilt ... guide you into all truth ... and tell you what is to come" (John 16:1 and 13). There is no mystery in His God-breathed presence. Learning in truth goes hand in hand with learning in spirit. When we enroll in the school of the Spirit, we open ourselves to the largess of His presence, breathing life into every fiber of our being.

Everyone has had the experience of being with someone whose spirit awed us. After Ken Taylor completed his work on *The Living Bible*, he welcomed me to his modest office with gentle grace, whispered with a stammering tongue, and then drove us to lunch in an aging auto with a rusty coat hanger for an antenna. There was no pretense in these humble signs. His spirit so enwrapped me that even now I remember being in the presence of a man of the Spirit. As we say in the drizzly Northwest, "When you stand on the corner in Seattle mist, you may not think it is raining, but you cannot stand there long before you are thoroughly drenched." The misty beauty of the God-breathed life is unmistakable.

Learning in grace. With the Word as our text and the Holy Spirit as our teacher, we open ourselves to a curriculum so tough that it will either make us or break us. We learn in the most practical way. We are taught the faith, rebuked for error, corrected for deviations, and trained in righteousness. Our natural response is to anticipate the teaching of faith and the training in righteousness but avoid being rebuked or corrected. Both the positive and the negative are part of the experience of maturing in grace. While the primary purpose of this discipline is to affirm orthodoxy and guard against heresy, the lessons apply to all of our experiences when the Holy Spirit is our teacher. Mature leaders are not born. They move toward maturity through the same rigors of teaching, rebuking, correcting, and training in their executive practice that they do in their Christian faith. Biographies of great leaders invariably reveal the highs of success and the lows of failure. Their greatness is defined because they kept success in perspective and learned from failure. In fact, most of them will say that they learned more from failure than from success. A CEO who never admits being wrong or refuses to accept correction is in trouble. Consultants can get right to the heart of the issue by asking, "What did you learn from it?" A leader who thinks deeply about the question and comes up with insightful answers will not only avoid repetition of the problem but will gain a chunk of practical wisdom that is indispensable in the maturation process. Jesus is our example. Hebrews 5:8-9b reads, "Although he was a son, he learned obedience through suffering and, once made perfect, he became the source of eternal salvation for all who obey him…" No one, not even Christ, comes to maturity without the rigors of obedience.

Our Maturing Model

Effective teaching puts the pieces of learning together in the life of the learner. In educational jargon, holistic learning leads to whole persons. Scripture makes the same claim. A *whole* person of God, *thoroughly* equipped, and doing *every* good work is the educator's dream. None of us dares to assume we have reached this ideal, but all of us can sense the energizing power of this promise for a lifetime of learning. Likewise, the board of a Christ-centered organization cannot expect its executive to fulfill this scriptural ideal, but it can expect to see its leader moving toward this model of maturity over time. Evidence comes as the leader shows gains in becoming a whole man or woman of God, thoroughly equipped, and doing every good work.

Maturing in character. Leaders of Christ-centered organizations have many titles to recognize their authority, such as CEO, general manager, or executive director. They may also have the added designations of Doctor or Reverend. To be honored as a "person of God," however, cannot be ascribed by human authority or earned by formal schooling. It must be learned by obedience to the Word of God, following the leadings of the Holy Spirit, and gaining wisdom from the lessons of experience. These are the pieces that come together to making the "whole" person of God. The Apostle Paul sees that vision in Romans 8:19 when he writes, "All creation stands on tiptoe watching the sons of God come into their own" (Phillips' Translation). The board of a Christ-centered organization can sense that same excitement as they watch their CEO move toward the identity of a "Man of God" or a "Woman of God." The best evidence that defines the character of a leader is in a singleness of purpose centered in God.

James Hudson Taylor III followed in the footsteps of his great grand-father, Hudson Taylor, as executive director of Overseas Missions Fellowship (formerly China Inland Mission) by giving 54 years of his life in ministry to the Chinese people. He died in 2009 with several titles and many degrees, but the one title that set him apart was given by Chinese Christians who called him a hard-boiled egg. "Many Chinese are bananas," they said, "Yellow on the outside, but white on the inside. You, however, are a hard-boiled egg, white on the outside, but yellow on the inside." At his memorial services in Hong Kong, Beijing, and Taiwan, they called him a Man of God because of his Godly love for the Chinese people." Even in his final days, James Hudson Taylor III was sending appeals across the world on behalf of the victims of the tragic Szechuan earthquake in February, 2009, that took thousands of victims including hundreds from the schools related to his ministry. He is our maturing model for the Man of God.

Maturing in competence. If a CEO ever stops learning the equipping skills of competency in leadership, the game is over. At the age of 80, I feel just about ready to assume a position of top leadership in a Christ-centered organization. Strange words from a person who became a college president at the age of 31? Not if we take seriously the words of Scripture. To be *thoroughly equipped* for leadership is a large order. CEOs of Christ-centered organizations answer the call of God with full knowledge that their competence is incomplete. Natural gifts have to be refined by executive experience and professional skills have to be tested against the demands of critical incidents. In my case, personal ambition, presidential position and professional preparation raced ahead of my spiritual development. It wasn't until retirement that I slowed down and stepped back so my soul could catch up with the driving forces of my mind and my will. Yet as I look back on my presidential career, I realize that the

Spirit of God became my "equipping agent" for each new challenge that confronted me. Competence is not a gift given in a moment. Nor is it the result of a hypothetical learning experience to prepare us for the future. Until we experience the suffering that goes along with obedience, we learn nothing.

The board of a Christ-centered organization will have no trouble observing the growth of its CEO in executive competence. New challenges come daily to test the creativity of executive leadership. A maturing leader will flex with the challenge and respond with an appropriate style; a stilted leader will fall back on old responses that numb the issue and stymie creativity. So the question for the board to ask is "How does our leader respond to new challenges?" Competence is not a fixed set of skills, but a flexible response to the surprising and the unexpected. Only with the gift of discernment from the Spirit of God can a leader meet the challenge.

Maturing of consequences. When the board evaluates its executive leadership, the review must go beyond success to consequences. Success is limited to accomplishing specific work goals checked off on the to-do list. Consequences, however, get into the quality of the work and its implications for the long-term. When Paul describes the end result of *"a man of God, thoroughly equipped for every good work,"* he is speaking of consequences beyond success. Good works have divine and human dimensions. To be good, they must be within the will of God; they must be filled with truth and grace; they must be merciful, humble and loving; they must give the glory to God. These standards for judgment apply especially to CEOs of Christ-centered organizations whose decisions and actions must be good to be godly.

Consequences also have long-term implications for policies and precedents. An expedient move may temporarily resolve an issue, but it can come back to bite the perpetrator. In one case, a board met to finalize arrangements for its leader who was moving to another position. When he was hired, the board authorized a large loan for him to buy a home in a high real estate market. The agreement included the clause that he would pay back the loan if he left the position. One very successful, self-made businessman moved that the loan be forgiven as an expression of gratitude for his ministry of five or so years. Another board member objected, saying this action would set a precedent for other staff who also had housing loans. "Bunk," the other board member reacted. "In my business, I do what I want and never worry about precedent." Such decisions, whether made by the board or its CEO, do need to be weighed for their long-term consequences as well as their immediate benefit to the person or persons involved. "Good works" will meet both criteria.

The holistic nature of maturity comes back again in the outcome that "every" work will be "good." We are now reaching out to new dimensions of leadership as change takes place within the Christ-centered organization and in its changing environment. Boards and their leaders will sometimes have knee-jerk reactions to the latest organizational fad or make hasty decisions to keep up with the competition. Maturing CEOs will stay abreast of the field without sacrificing the values of "good work" according to biblical principles.

Our maturing model gives every board of a Christ-centered organization reason to fulfill its sacred trust by nurturing its CEO. Board members find personal satisfaction in answering the call of God to serve as a steward for all of His resources. These include developing policies of good governance to guide the organization, sharing a faith commitment with colleagues of like mind, building a redemptive ministry in the name of Jesus Christ and representing that ministry in the church, community and public-at-large. But there is no greater satisfaction than to be part of a learning organization and a partner with a maturing CEO. Nurturing the CEO is the highest order of business for the board of a Christ-centered organization. To see our leader maturing as a whole man or woman of God, thoroughly equipped for every good work—this is our sacred trust.

With All Due Diligence
Board Check
Maturing Model

With personal, professional and spiritual maturity as the board's goal for CEO nurture, do you see your leader:

	Yes	No
1. growing in understanding and application of the whole Word of God;	_____	_____
2. being quickened by the Spirit of God in all dimensions of life;	_____	_____
3. learning practical wisdom from the disciplines of the Word and the Spirit;	_____	_____
4. maturing in character as a whole man or woman of God;	_____	_____
5. maturing in competence as a fully prepared professional; and	_____	_____
6. maturing in consequences that assure long-term quality and contribute to a vision of the whole.	_____	_____

David L. McKenna

50 Years in Christian Higher Education

Dr. David McKenna has served for more than 50 years in Christian higher education, including 33 years as a college, university and seminary president.

At Spring Arbor College (now University), he developed a junior college into a four-year Christian liberal arts college; at Seattle Pacific University, he led the transition from a four-year college to university status; at Asbury Theological Seminary, he gained and guided the largest grant ever given in American history to a free standing graduate school of theology. In 1994, Dr. McKenna retired as President Emeritus of Asbury Theological Seminary to write, speak and consult on subjects related to leadership in Christian higher education and ministry. In 2003, he retired as Chair Emeritus, Board of Trustees, Spring Arbor University.

Dr. McKenna holds a B.A. degree in History from Western Michigan University, Master of Divinity from Asbury Theological Seminary, and an M.A. in Counseling Psychology and Ph.D. in Higher Education from the University of Michigan.

He has been awarded ten honorary doctorates, named as a Paul Harris Fellow with Rotary International, and honored by Stanley Kresge's endowment for the David L. McKenna Christian Leaders Scholarship for business students at Seattle Pacific University.

McKenna's presidencies have been recognized at Seattle Pacific University by the David L. McKenna Hall for the School of Business, at Asbury Theological Seminary by the David and Janet McKenna Chapel, and at Spring Arbor University by the David and Janet Carillon Tower. As an educational leader, he served as Founding Chair for the Christian College Consortium (parent organization of the Council of Christian Colleges & Universities) and Secretary for the National Association of Independent Colleges and Universities.

In 1980, he was a finalist for Secretary of Education in the Reagan Cabinet. As a religious leader ordained in the Free Methodist Church, McKenna has held positions as Vice President of the World Methodist Council, Consulting Editor for Christianity Today, and a national radio commentator. In civic leadership, he chaired Governor Dan Evan's select committee to study gambling in the State of Washington and was honored as First Citizen of Seattle in 1976.

A prolific writer, Dr. McKenna is the author of 32 books that range across the fields of psychology, biblical commentary, leadership, history and theology.

The McKennas celebrate their 60th wedding anniversary in 2010. They are parents of four children, 12 grandchildren, and one great-grandchild.

DAVID L. MCKENNA

CEO Selection,
Transition and
Development for Boards
of Christ-centered Organizations

Stewards
of a
SACRED
TRUST

stewardsofasacredtrust.com

ECFA
PRESS

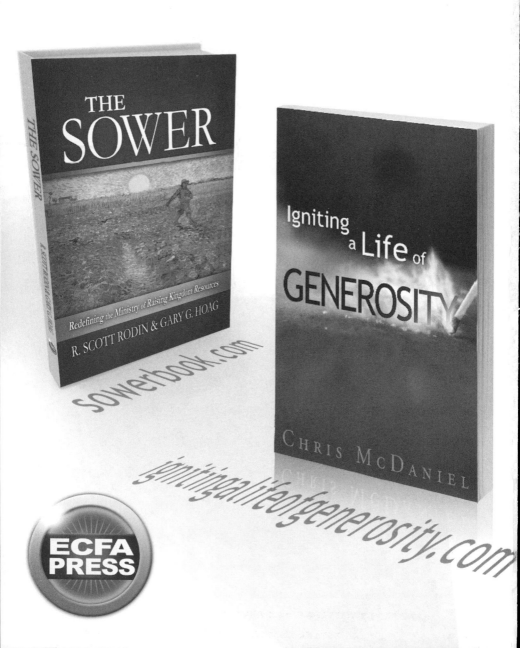